WUSSIE

In Praise of
Spineless Men

Josh Muggins

About the Author

By the Author

This isn't my first book. I'm not going to tell you the titles of the other two because I'm afraid that you will find them, read them, dislike them, and then publicly say or write mean things about them.

Your hypothetical cruel words actually should not wound me, since "Josh Muggins" is not even my real name but merely a coy *nom de plume* that I employ as a buffer between myself and a heartless, critical world. And yet such is the state of my psyche that even this pseudonym provides only a limited protection, rather like those bulletproof vests that the heroes of Eighties action blockbusters were always secretly wearing that allowed them to survive a dying villain's last Uzi barrage, but only at the price of bruised ribs and a long, suspenseful, death-like unconsciousness that persisted until an overwrought costar, whom the hero had initially treated with sexist disdain until she gained his respect and shared his bodily fluids, shook the hero's shoulders while bellowing something along the lines of "Dammit, Miller! Don't you die on me! *You hear me? Don't you die on me!!*"

You know, like that.

I will confide in you this far: My earlier books were, like this one, self-published. This is not, as you might expect, because I suffered rejection at the hands of innumerable publishers and agents. In fact, no publisher or literary agent ever glimpsed the manuscripts of those earlier books, in large part because I so deeply feared suffering rejection at their hands, no matter how brief and perfunctory those rejections would surely have been.

As you can see, this "wussie" business is no mere gimmick with me; it is a way of life. So if you have anything to tell me about this book, mean or otherwise, I hope you'll tell me privately at the address below.

Be gentle.

joshmuggins@hotmail.com

www.joshmuggins.com

CONTENTS

INTRODUCTION TO THE PAPERBACK EDITION

After three and a half years of "research" and writing, I self-published this opus as an ebook in January 2011 with every intention of bringing it out as a "book-book" within that year.

Six weeks later, my country of residence was shaken, sloshed, and irradiated in a triple-whammy disaster that you may remember hearing about and, well…you have to admit, as excuses for procrastination go, that one holds up pretty well.

In editing this paperback version, I have resisted temptation to alter the contents apart from edits necessitated by the change of format and the correction of a few errors—I can't believe I pushed a product out into the world that refers to Richard I as "the Lionhear*ted*" (my brethren and sistren in the League of Extraordinary Copy Editors will understand)—but I fear that you readers of the mid-teens will be baffled by some of my turn-of-the-millennium references.

I started the book at a time when the reality show *The Osbournes* was still a pretty fresh memory for perhaps everyone except its own star, a time when Ralph Macchio was the one and only Karate Kid, a time when sex toys for men simply were not discussed, a time when Alan Colmes still served a purpose as a comedic punching bag—which is to say, a time when Alan Colmes served a purpose. (Oh, look there: a rare act of wussie-on-wussie violence.) Such moldy references will, I fear, be lost on younger readers.

Occasionally, I even erred the other way, *under*estimating the longevity of a social phenomenon, as when I addressed readers of the distant future (2015) to explain just exactly who "the late" Lindsay Lohan had been. My apologies to Lindsay—may she outlive me and my ilk. Especially the ilk.

Anyway, long story short, I remember the rabid outcry that greeted George Lucas when he started monkeying around with his first batch of *Star Wars* episodes and thought, "Who needs all that grief?" So I have opted to leave everything in *Wussie: In Praise of Spineless Men* as it was. Thus, those of you who missed your chance to ignore the release of the ebook can now enjoy this opportunity to ignore a wholly new version, safe in the knowledge that you are ignoring the same content that your grandfather thrilled to ignoring lo those many years ago.

Josh Muggins
September 2014

The whole of existence frightens me.

— Søren Kierkegaard

1. Name that Film: An Exercise

Sorry to go all Malcolm Gladwell on you right out of the gate here, but I'd like to start off by asking you to try a short quiz. Below are summaries of three well-known films. A key detail or two has been altered in each one. Can you identify the movies despite the changes?*

A

Dave (Adam Sandler) is a homosexual, but through a series of zany mix-ups on a cross-country flight he is wrongly accused of sexually harassing a female flight attendant and is ordered to undergo therapy. His irritating therapist, Buddy (Jack Nicholson), insinuates himself into every aspect of Dave's life, forcing him to confront the fact that his gayness is impeding his personal and professional growth. With Buddy's help, Dave eventually overcomes his homosexuality and begins to lead a happy and fulfilling heterosexual life.

B

Jack (Edward Norton), a thirty-something devout Jew, is a low-

---

* Yes, you can.

level employee for an automobile company. His Torah-centric life is so unsatisfying that he suffers from chronic insomnia. On a business trip he befriends Tyler (Brad Pitt). After Jack loses his home, Tyler agrees to put him up, but only if Jack will subscribe to Tyler's muscular brand of Christianity. Jack agrees, and the two establish an underground network of "Jesus Clubs" and set about aggressively luring other despondent Jews into their fold. Shaking off the shackles of Yahweh, Jack feels fulfilled for the first time in his life.

C

Daniel (Will Smith), a shy and skinny light-skinned black teenager, moves with his mother to a California suburb. After he is seen talking to a white girl (Elizabeth Shue), he is set upon by a gang of Caucasian boys led by her ex-boyfriend (William Zabka). The scene is witnessed by a wise old Asian-American man (Pat Morita) who has faced and overcome similar treatment at the hands of the community. He takes Daniel under his wing and trains him to cast aside his black identity and learn to "act white," as he himself has done. Thanks to his mentor's coaching, Daniel wins the respect of the Aryan gangsters and the love of the girl.

I'm sure you had little trouble discerning that the movies in question are *Anger Management* (aka "that Sandler and Nicholson comedy that should have been better"), *Fight Club*, and *The Karate Kid* (original 1984 version). You have further noticed that a parallel alteration has been made to each movie's storyline—a twist so diabolical that not even Gladwell's warped mind could have concocted it.

Adam Sandler's character in *Anger Management* is not gay; he's a weak-willed man—a "wussie," one might say. It is not his homosexuality that he overcomes in the course of the movie, then, but his "wussitude."

Similarly, Jack in *Fight Club* suffers not from his religious affiliation but from his inability to assert himself, which he likewise rises above thanks to his fateful encounter with Tyler.

And of course, the protagonist of *The Karate Kid* is portrayed by young Ralph Macchio, not young Will Smith. The plot has nothing to do with the hero's race and everything to do with his helplessness against bullies—a "failing" that he conquers with the aid of karate master Mr. Miyagi.

Here's my point: Suppose that these movies really had been made and released with the plots that I have outlined. Every American to the left of a well-lubed Mel Gibson would have been outraged, and rightly so. Theaters showing such intolerant tripe would have been picketed, and rightly so. Acts of violence against theater owners might have been threatened, and perhaps understandably so. We celebrate our nation's diversity and cringe at the notion that homosexuality, Judaism and blackness are debilities to be overcome.

Why, then, do we not also celebrate, or at least accept, the congenital spinelessness so prevalent in today's boys and men? Why, then, is wussitude treated as a weed that must be rooted from a youngster's soul? Isn't this condition every bit as integral to his identity as his race, creed, and sexual preference? Isn't this condition, too, received by chance and not by choice? No one asks to be born a wussie, to be condemned to a life of ridicule in his PE classes, of knock-kneed awkwardness in his romantic entanglements, of powerless obscurity in his writing career. Yet we are programmed to believe that this is a condition that can and ought to be "treated" and "cured."

Admit it: You cheered when the Sandler and Norton characters faced up to their respective obnoxious bosses, and when Daniel-san single-handedly mowed down the entire Cobra Kai. How do you think such storylines made us unreconstructed wussies feel? Did you even give us a passing thought?

Now, look, I know what you're thinking. This is new territory for most of you, tolerance-wise. *What? Are you serious?* you may well be wondering right now. *Do you actually expect us to consider the plight of gutless pushovers in the same light as the plights of African-Americans, Jews, gays and lesbians—groups with long histories of agonizing struggle against very real and often deadly discrimination?*

And do you know what? I'll tell you what. I will look you straight in the eye and give you my answer. My answer is:

It depends.

It depends on whether or not you are really, really angry with me for having concocted this analogy. If you are, then no, I'm not serious. Really. I'm not.

Ha-ha. Just kidding. Forget I ever brought this up. Really.

Stop glaring like that.

Please.

Cut a wussie some slack, won't you?

2. Another Day in Wussie Paradise

I needed to write this book, you see, after belatedly coming to grips with my lifelong wussitude. That epiphany seems as good a place as any to start, so I hope you'll indulge me by sitting right back and hearing my tale, a tale of a fateful trip. It started from a tropic port, as these things are wont to do...

—◻—

It starts, in fact, one bright morning at the bus stop in front of the Royal Kuhio in Waikiki. I'm stopping here for four nights in September 2007, ostensibly to attend an academic conference at the University of Hawaii, and am on my way to the famed Ala Moana Shopping Center.

So here I am in my favorite dark blue hibiscus-print aloha shirt and regulation white shorts and sandals and my Milwaukee Brewers cap, ensconced on a wooden bench amid the blobs of Hawaiian sunshine that trickle between the fronds of the tall palms.

I should take a brief aside here to explain that I am no Brewers fan. It's just that trial and error has established the cap of the Milwaukee Brewers, a team that has left such faint and dainty footprints on Major League Baseball history in its four-decade existence as to arouse the enmity of no rival fan base, as the ideal scalp accessory for one of my temperament. Don a Brewers cap, and even the most florid and pot-bellied of SportsCenter junkies can only squint at the thing, flip quickly through his memory files in search of just cause to accost you, come up empty, and then turn away, dismissing cap and wearer with a single world-weary snort.

Of course, one could always go capless, couldn't one? But no, one couldn't. You see, I live and work in Japan, and am bald. Neither of these conditions is damning in and of itself, but in combination they are as provocative as the proverbial fart in a spacesuit, for baldness is considered endlessly comical in Japan. Thus, I must wear a cap of some sort while commuting to work or risk the scorn of adolescent schoolgirls. So the Brewers hat becomes a habit even on visits to the good old Great Satan.

Anyway, here I sit in my vacation-in-paradise wardrobe, trying desperately to project carefree island-boy laid-backedness. A smug sense of seniority washes over me as I watch my fellow tourists try to decipher the bus routes and fares. Mrs. Muggins and I have been annual visitors to the Islands for some years by this time—have even purchased a small condo in town as an investment property in a mad outburst of derring-do. And now the bus arrives, putting the agitated newbies out of their misery.

The interior of "The Bus"—for that is what Honoluluites have cunningly named their municipal transportation system—radiates all the tropical gaiety of an autopsy room on a police forensics drama. At the very front are two long benches facing each other, and I snag a seat at the end of one. To occupy one of the forward-facing seats further back, I know from bitter experience, is to risk getting boxed in by a fellow passenger and perhaps having to make small talk.

Directly across from me sits a skinny middle-aged blonde lady who, I sense, has selected her seat through an identical neighbor-avoidance strategy. To her right, a matched set of middle-aged Japanese ladies occupies the frontmost of the forward-facing seats in edgy silence. (See Figure 1)

Silent bus...holy bus... My sphincter slowly uncurls and I begin to mentally map out my plan of attack for the shopping center. I will beeline for the bookstore and then browse for a gift for Mrs. Muggins, and then head back to my room after what should be, at most, a three-hour tour.

A three-hour tour...

—◻—

I can say it now: My name is Josh, and I'm a wussie. Well, my name isn't really Josh. But a wussie I most definitely am.

Actually, what I am is that word that begins with P and rhymes with wussie, the word for which wussie *was created as a euphemism. In this book, for fear of offending readers, I will eschew the P-word except when quoting others, which I will probably do every chance I get just for the vicarious thrill of typing the P-word, thus making me, as you can see, not only a wussie but a bit of a weasel to boot.*

I'm not sure exactly when my weaseliness kicked in, but I'm pretty sure I've been a wussie all my life. Like most of the tribe, I lived in denial of my wussitude for many years before grudgingly acknowledging it. Wussitude, like gayness or a genuine appreciation of the Twilight *novels, is not an aspect of a young man's identity that he can easily make his peace with.*

To make matters worse, wussies have no support group, no community. And no wussie pride parades, for the obvious reason that no one would march in one. Wussies just aren't into all that flamboyance, that whole business of getting together and chanting "We're here, we're queer, get used to it!" or "Out of the closet and into the streets!" Our rallying cry would be something along the lines of: "We're here. But we'll go over there if you prefer." And you can rest assured you will never in your life hear the sotto voce *admonition, "Steer clear of that joint if you know what's good for you. It's a wussie bar."*

No, one does not embrace one's wussitude easily. And when one finally does, it is apt to be that sort of tentative embrace that bitter primary rivals spring on each other during the final night of their party's nominating convention. Wussitude has a way of looming in on one like a seriously pissed off John McCain bounding stiffly out of the shadows with a scarily fake smile plastered across his face. No sane man willingly embraces something like that. Yet in order to survive and thrive, embrace it we must.

7

—▢—

In the middle of the next block the doors whoosh open in front of another condo complex and the bus gobbles up another viscous clot of floral-printed visitors. Skinny Blonde Lady recoils at the prospect of the adjacent seat being occupied by God knows who; my sphincter contracts in sympathy.

Prominent among the horde of God-knows-whos boarding here are a boisterous couple in their sixties with Australian accents, immediately identifiable as the type of folks who put the *public* in *public transportation*. The wife sits to my right, and the husband, clad in a brilliant powder-blue aloha shirt and white shorts, plops his dry-roasted self down next to my ally, good old SBL, who cringes.

The intruder loudly begins to brief his wife on the information re transfers and routes that he has just extracted from the driver, then segues seamlessly into the broader theme of how *guh-RITE* it is to be here in Hawaii on this *luvvly dye*, remarks which, augmented by his expansive arm gestures and swiveling head, immediately pull all of us within an eight-foot radius into his orbit. His grin opens an irrigation system of deep, curvy crinkles across his desiccated face, which is capped by an unfairly full head of snow-white hair. A line from a novelty song popular in my youth plays on a loop in my head:

Tan me hide when I'm dead, Fred.

Poor Skinny Blonde Lady looks as if she has just discovered the contents of Norman Bates's basement, and who can blame her? Her space bubble has been invaded by this quintessential God-Knows-Who, this mummified descendant of convicts—of people cast out of England by the English for speaking in an accent too outrageous even for them. But there is nothing I can do.

By this time the intruder has launched into a freestyle treatise on his previous visit to the "Stoits" a few years back. He and "the missus" visited Alaska in winter on that occasion, which he found "a wee bit cooler than it is 'ere."

"Just a wee bit, eh?" says Skinny Blonde Lady, at which moment a little piece of me dies. I unfurl my PennySaver, a free tabloid full of used car ads and clippable coupons that I grabbed at the supermarket as a firewall against just this sort of outbreak of conviviality. Ah, Skinny Blonde Lady, I thought I knew you.

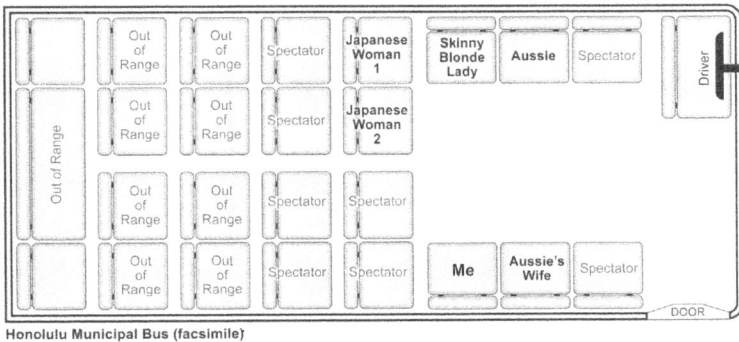

Honolulu Municipal Bus (facsimile)

Figure 1: A rough schematic of seating on the intra-city bus from Waikiki to Ala Moana, approximately 10 a.m., September 17, 2007.

"*Eh-aooou!*" says Aussie Man, christening a spanking new diphthong for service in the English language, "I'm glad to see you got a sense a' humor on you!"

"Oh, yeah," she replies, now fully uncoiled. "Ohh, yeah! A big one!" As proof, she adds, "*Ah-ha-ha-ha-ha-ha-ha-ha!*"

This encourages Aussie Man to launch into an anecdote about the trip to Anchorage, a *luvvly* city, he assures us.

"I've never been," interjects Blondie the Betrayer, "but I hear it's more beautiful than Fairbanks."

"Beautiful, oh my yes, I should say so! But too cold for my taste."

"A big baby, he is," chimes in Mrs. Aussie, bringing the conflagration dangerously close in.

"Well, I've always said that someone ought to nurse me," he

replies on cue, "preferably a woman!" which sets off another screechy demonstration of Blondie's famously expansive sense of humor.

Great, I mutter into a picture of a '96 Honda Civic, now he's been sanctioned to work blue.

"May I ask where you're from?" says Aussie Man to Blondie. "The South—that's what I'm thinkin'."

"From Alabama, originally!" she replies with delight. "But I lost the accent." Then she repeats herself—*Ah lawwwst the ah-yuk-sint*—just for a laugh, which she promptly provides: "*AH-HA-HA-HA-HA-HA-HA!*"

Others seated in the vicinity begin to eye Blondie with a sort of benign envy, for clearly our charismatic leader has elevated her to Official Sidekick. These onlookers include the two Japanese ladies, who have little idea what is being said but smile and nod anyway while conferring in whispers behind palms.

"I remember there were these two middle-aged Japanese ladies on the tour," says Aussie Man, perhaps inspired by the presence of these doppelgangers. "And you know how dour and serious they can be, right?"

Blondie giggles. Oh yes, she knows exactly what he means, she says. So, evidently, do our own Japanese ladies, who continue to smile and nod.

"But these ladies, they were just as nice as could be! And one of them, I remember, was bundled up in all these layers of clothes, all nice and snug, but then found it was a wee bit warm on the tour bus. So she tried to take off the top layer. Only it was too crowded on the bus so she was havin' a spot o' trouble. Then I stepped up and helped 'er out of 'er coat. And she smiled and said thank you. Then she wanted to take off the next layer, a *cahh*-di-gan, and I helped 'er with that, too, and she said thank you..."

Only forty thousand miles on that Civic, it says. Hmm, that's dubious...

"And then I just stood there till she looked at me, and I said —"

"You said, 'Keep going'! *AH-HA-HA-HA-HA-HA-HA-HA-HA!*"

Irritation flickers across Aussie Man's face like heat lightning. His sycophants miss it, but it's clear that this is a man who does *not* appreciate having his punch lines stepped on. He presses on:

"No, no! I just pointed to her dress and I said, 'Next?' And she looked at me like—" (Here he mimes slow comprehension followed by eye-popping dread.) "And then she says, 'Oh! *No-no-no-no-no-no!*'"

"Because," his wife adds helpfully, "that was her last layer!"

"She wasn't wearin' nothin' under it!"

Normally I'm a sucker for scenarios, real or hypothetical, involving the disrobing of Japanese women, and yet I cannot share in the general mirth spreading like a gas leak through the front half of the bus. Over Aussie Man's shoulder and across the highway, sparks of morning sunlight dance on blue ocean waves, providing an apt visual accompaniment to the tinkling laughter of my fellow passengers, while I wrestle somberly with my options. Should I smile and nod and laugh along? What if Aussie Man decides to call on me, then? "So what's your story, mate?" he might ask. "Findin' any *bahhgains* in that shopper, are we?" And oh, wouldn't *that* set Blonde Ed McMahon off…

Or should I crouch behind my paper shield, tight-lipped, and risk the enmity of my peers? One could imagine Aussie Man and his wife dropping in a pub at the shopping center for a ten a.m. bracer. "That was a *guh-rite* crowd on the bus, just *guh-RITE!*" he would enthuse. "Except…did you see that one feller? Just kept lookin' a' his li'l ol' newspaper? Never cracked a smile?"

"Never moind, dear. Never moind," his wife would coo, patting his leathery forearm. "You did your best. There's like to be one o' that koind on every bus, I reckon."

I try to banish such thoughts and focus instead on the garage-kept, excellent condition '91 Lexus that a guy in Waipaho wants to unload. And look here: a towing service offers rates as low as $40! That's good to know, because Lord knows I could never bring myself to blame the former owner for my own failure to get the car re-started once I had driven it off his property.

—◻—

That afternoon, safely back in my room, I call the septuagenarian property manager who is handling our condo. I haven't seen her for two and a half years. She has kept the unit occupied and the rent checks flowing in, but since the last time we met in person she has been hospitalized twice, first for injuries suffered in a traffic accident and later after a fall. Thus, it's essential that I get her to sit down with me face to face so that I can determine whether or not the time has come to replace her.

Should I decide to keep her on, I will need to be firm with her regarding email etiquette. It's not that she is computer illiterate. Any inquiry I make is followed by a prompt response. It's just that said response invariably takes the form of forwarded lists of jokes and heartwarming homilies that she has received from friends and family, without reference to my question.

And though it's not a high priority, I hope I can also impress upon her once and for all my desire to be addressed as "Josh." Her habit of calling me "Joshua" tends to reinforce in my mind the unnerving resemblance she bears to my seventh-grade social studies teacher, another grandmotherly, yellow-permed, no-nonsense, jiggly-jowled juggernaut who cowed me at will.

As I dial, I recall how impressed I was the first time I met her. She was everything one could want in a property manager. No tenant would be able to defy this blue-eyed battle-axe. It didn't occur to me then that this might apply to clients as well.

Me: Hello, June? It's Josh. I'm in town for a visit.

June: Josh? [Long pause] Ah, Joshua! It took me a while to place you.

Me: Ha-ha. Sorry about that. Anyway, I'm in town for five days. I, uh, I told you by email I'd be coming.

June: Oh, did you? Well, welcome back. When did you get in?

Me: Yesterday. I came for an English teachers' conference.

June: An English teachers' conference? What do you mean? What kind of conference is that?

Me: Well, it's a conference. For teachers. Of English. You know, teachers of English to speakers of other languages.

June: So... I don't get this. Do they all come from Japan? Or from around here?

Me: I expect there'll be people from all around the world, especially places where English is taught as a foreign language: Japan, Europe, South America...

June: Well, that sounds fascinating! But that starts from the nineteenth, didn't you say?

Not for the first time do I note what a remarkably selective memory the woman has. Lost in the ether are the purpose of my visit, what I do for a living, and exactly who I am. But the starting date of my conference? Right on the tip of her tongue.

Me: Yes, but...anyway, my university pays for it, so I thought I'd come early. Besides, I don't really plan to attend the conference all that much. Just show up to register for it and, then, you know, heh, do whatever I want.

June: So, what are you going to do, then?

Me: I—I don't know.

June: Is your family with you?

Me: No. Michiko and I were planning to come together but then she had a conflict at the last minute.

June: Well, I should think you'd go to the conference then. Otherwise, what do you have to do...

    ...but fall in with the WRONG CROWD again, Joshua? fills in the ghostly voice of Mrs. McGunnell, the late social studies teacher.

Me: Yeah... Yeah, I guess you're right. I suppose I will end up attending most of it.

June: Well, I should think so!

    Crap, I'm thinking. Now I'll actually have to go to the stupid thing so that I can answer her questions about it later.

Me: Anyway, I was hoping I could meet you and go over some things tomorrow morning or sometime on Friday.

June: Well, the apartment's been rented. A nice couple came to see me; they'd just been married. The bride was still in her wedding dress!

Me: Oh, really?

June: So it's rented for twelve-fifty… How's the weather been in Japan, Joshua?

This question, I will realize all too late, is a Trojan horse designed to allow June access yet again to one of her favorite themes, i.e. her trip to Japan many years ago and the awful sweet-cakes she had to consume as part of a traditional tea ceremony, and how a Japanese woman, a friend of a friend, took care of her in Kobe, and did she mention the sweet-cakes?

All the while, my free ear picks up the sounds of happy Waikiki tourists having loads of fun on the streets below. A few floors down, I visualize the Royal Kuhio swimming pool coolly glimmering in the mid-afternoon sun, its perimeter lined with young American women slathering thick globs of sunscreen all over themselves.

But I keep listening as June reminds me yet again of the Kobe woman's American husband who had lived there for years and was so very fluent in Japanese, as I probably am not because I am obviously such a hoser. June is Canadian, so I assume that *hoser* would be her internal monologue's epithet of choice for me. It is around this point in the conversation that I realize that I do not really need to meet with her if I can just get some assurance of her well-being.

Me: So…how have you been?

June: Oh, I'm fine. Had some nasty double-whiplash in that car crash. And then that fall on top of everything else! It was my wrist, you know…

Five minutes later I am satisfied re her ability to go forward as my representative. If her phone stamina is any indication of her overall vitality, I must be in good hands. I inform her I have changed my mind regarding our meeting as, per her advice, I'll

15

soon be too busy enjoying all those exhilarating conference presentations on corpus linguistics and syllabus design all day, every day, for the rest of my entire stay, and indeed might even go up to the conference site this very evening just to soak up the ambience and watch the organizing committee put up signage and posters.

I check email as soon as I get off the phone and find a new message from June titled "Fwd: TRULY SPECTACULAR: THIS IS AWSOME!"

—◻—

Life as lived by a wussie is not unexciting, if only because our thresholds for excitement are so low. A trace of blood on a steak or a random glimpse of cleavage on an elevator provides us with the same adrenaline rush that an ordinary person would have to ascend a major Himalayan peak solo to achieve. We wussies save a lot on airfare.

A state of mind that renders such mundane occurrences thrilling ought to be a consummation devoutly to be wished, but most of us could do without it, frankly. The sudden quickening of the heart rate, the rusty taste of fear in the gullet, the Maw of Oblivion opening before one's eyes—that crap gets old when you experience it six times before lunch on a Wednesday, let me tell you.

If you think about it, the very existence of wussies in our modern world is a miracle. Evolution was supposed to have long ago selected our pasty asses out of existence. It's really rather shocking that Creationists haven't held us up to bolster their claims.

Think of it this way: Suppose that human societies had evolved so that only a few elite males were shared as mates among all the females—as is the case in some primate species and Big Ten schools. If we humans had followed the model of Japanese macaques, for example, the closest someone like me could ever manage to get to any real action today would be the privilege of untangling burrs from my Leader's back-hair while he drills one of my sisters from behind. In such a scenario, the Wussie Gene would have long since died out.

Of course, all things being relative, there would still be varying levels of macho in such a hypothetical society, but the gamut would only run from your

16

mixed martial arts champions at the top down to, say, a Hugh Jackman or a Robert Pattinson at the bottom. There would be no George Stephanopolouses, no Ben Quayles. If an early Woody Allen comedy could be imported into this imaginary universe, all the males would be mystified by the first several minutes of it. Then they would furiously dash the projector to the floor and gnaw the shards.*

How, then, did we get here? My suspicion is this: At some point during the Dawn of Man, females convened a summit and arrived at a momentous consensus that subsequent generations of their sex have regretted. They decided that their loathing for wussies, great as it was, was trumped by their loathing for sharing the few acceptable males. "Some of you girls are going to have to bite the bullet on this one," some proto-biker chick proclaimed. "It's time we spread the wealth around."

And in that fateful moment, Monogamy was born and wussies—at least the more presentable among them—were enabled to pass on their piss-poor sniveling excuse for genes and perpetuate their ilk, leading inexorably to me and Alan Colmes.

—□—

That night I do not meander to the conference site. Instead I go for a walk around eleven, a stroll that takes me along Kuhio and up and down the perpendicular streets that connect Kuhio to Kalakaua. As any Honoluluite can tell you, a stroll on these streets at this time of the night is likely to bring the stroller into close proximity with streetwalkers.

---

* I don't count Woody Allen himself as a wussie—the man started out as a stand-up comic, for heaven's sake, and later survived a barrage of bad publicity that would have slaughtered a battalion of bona fide wussies— but he certainly made a lucrative career for himself *playing* wussies.

For what it's worth, my Pantheon of Wussie-Portraying Actors features (in rough chronological order) Stan Laurel, Bert "Cowardly Lion" Lahr, Larry Fine, Don Knotts, Jonathan "Dr. Smith" Harris, Werner "Col. Klink" Klemperer, Woody Allen, John "Fredo" Cazale, Anthony "C3PO" Daniels, Crispin "George McFly" Glover and Martin P. "Telly Monster" Robinson.

But I'm just curious. Just looking. Just out for a stroll. After all, Waikiki prostitutes are well known to be the Sumatran tigers of the sex industry—proud, breathtakingly beautiful and nearly always deadly. Their MO, or so a credible tourist guidebook informs me, is to lure the unsuspecting prey into a taxi and whisk him to their den of operations, where a quick wallet-ectomy will be performed *sans* anesthesia with no services given in exchange.

And that's the outcome if one is lucky. Another common scenario involves meeting up with a comely member of the Honolulu Police Department and subsequently having one's name published in the *Honolulu Star-Bulletin*, where one's property manager will see it, jiggle her jowls in disgust, and then forward the news along with one's mugshot to everyone she knows.

I'm strolling up Kaiulani back toward Kuhio, just looking. This seems to be Streetwalker Central, at least on this night. For someone who is just looking, I'm not really doing much looking; it suddenly occurs to me that actually looking—making eye contact—could result in an awkward misreading of my intentions. So I look at trees, the sidewalk, shops across the street as I shuffle along.

Suddenly I find myself between a long-legged Scandinavian closing in behind me and a pair of slow-moving Nubian princesses in front of me, in a variation of the "sandwiching" prank favored by bored semi-truck drivers on Midwestern stretches of Interstate. I must not be boxed in. I pass the slow-moving Nubian princesses on the grass.

"Want some chocolate?" inquires the darker of the two.

"No thank you," I mutter, in the tone of Tom Hanks in that movie where he plays a twelve-year-old boy trapped in a grown man's body. A puckish temptation to say, "Why, yes, I'd love some!"—and then escort the young lady to some open-air café and see how far I could get in ordering us some chocolate milk and cake—flits through my head. But I know I could never pull that off. A wussie's life is a life packed with such unhatched schemes—potentially great anecdotes that die in embryo.

"Hi!" says Chocolate Girl's more persistent mocha friend as I round the corner onto Kuhio. "Looking for some company?"

"No. No, thank you. I'm fine."

She's moving at a good clip now so I try to lag behind her. Then she stops to confer with a colleague so I pass her again, only to get stuck behind another slow-moving pair whom I don't want to pass for fear of calling attention to myself. In the meantime, I am accosted twice more:

"You up for a good time tonight?"

"You all alone, sugar?"

In a Bizarro world where it is dweebish middle-aged men who lurk on side streets to sell their favors to the self-loathing young bombshells passing by, what would my sales pitch be? "Hey there, honey! Looking for some vanilla gristle?" "You up for a thoroughly tedious time tonight?" I am pondering these and other slogans when Mocha Lass sidles up next to me again.

Mocha Lass: All these pretty girls on the street and you're just going to walk on by?

Me: I'm honestly just out for a walk tonight.

Mocha Lass: Hmm… Okay…

A pregnant pause follows as we walk along together: *Tiger, tiger, burning bright…*

Mocha Lass: You have a good night now.

Me: Thanks. You—you're very lovely.

Mocha Lass: Thank you!

On the way back to my room, I stop at an ABC convenience store to buy some ice cream that I don't want or need, just so the security guard at the Royal Kuhio can see me bringing something back and understand that I didn't go out to browse the hookers. He had looked askance at me on my way out. No, really. I'm sure he had.

— ¤ —

We've all had to read Sunrise at Campobello *at some point in our middle or high school careers, so we know the story of Franklin Roosevelt's heroic struggle to transcend the ravages of polio. We likewise know from the award-winning biopic that Ray Charles didn't let blindness slow him down. Helen Keller one-upped Ray by single-handedly whupping the Blindness-Deafness tag-team to become one of her era's most prominent socialist blowhards. All have been held up to the youth of America to inspire us to overcome our handicaps.*

Pop culture has even indoctrinated us to applaud those who wrangle with self-inflicted handicaps like drug addiction (Ray Charles again, Johnny Cash), or with invisible mental afflictions, like the guy Russell Crowe played in that one Ron Howard movie and, well, Ray Charles. Our hats also go off to those who run headlong into prejudice and don't give up (Mohammed Ali, Gandhi, Ray Charles), and those who rise from abject poverty to greatness (the guy Russell Crowe played in that other Ron Howard movie, and don't forget Ray Charles), and those who defy conventional thinking to create bold new forms of art (Jackson Pollock, and can I get an Amen for brother Ray Charles?).

Where, then, is the love for those who overcome the world's prejudice against wussitude? Where are our role models? Our biopics? Our roles for Russell Crowe?

— ¤ —

The following day I go to Starbucks for lunch again because I simply don't have the nerve to walk into a real sit-down restaurant without Michiko. And to think that twelve hours earlier I was contemplating buying a wholesome midnight snack for a working girl...

My server—or do they call them baristas now? Thank God I don't have to address him by his title... Anyway, it's the same guy I had yesterday, a chipper lad with hair like that Justin fellow from *American Idol* a few years back. For all I know, it could *be* Justin. Lest Justin think me a dullard, I eschew yesterday's selection of the turkey-egg sandwich and go with the sausage-egg, and in an even more audacious move, ditch the mocha frappuccino for a caramel one.

As I get settled in with my newspaper and lunch, a young buckaroo enters, yammering into his cell phone in a Texas accent. "Well, they recruited that hot shot running back, you know... Yep... And he took off up the sideline, and it looked like he was gonna score but... Hang on a second..."

He keeps milling around with the phone lodged between his flabby chin and shoulder as he preps his own frappuccino for take-out. This takes an inordinately long time. During the process, he veers toward me so as to flick items into the wastebox near my seat, causing me to flinch in the fear that he will steal my table from me or, even worse, occupy it with me while continuing his cell phone conversation. (Or worse still, terminate that conversation and try to begin a new one with me.)

Rattled, I make preparations to leave, but by the time I am heading for the door, so is he—still dissecting the inadequacies of his team's defense. Fortunately, he does not make toward my condo, for if he did, I would have to find some excuse to go the other way and circle the block because, well, that's just the way I roll...

—◻—

Back in my room, the afternoon stretches before me as bleak and uninviting as a Lars von Trier film festival. I've brought my computer with me in hopes of making a start on another book, but no ideas are coming. Last night, after my harrowing stroll, I needed three beers and a sleeping pill to bring myself down, and the aftereffects are impeding my concentration.

Like most writers, I drink and medicate more than I ought to because I'm besieged by demons, but in my case even the demons are wussies. I stick to beer and wine, no spirits; I ran out of prescription meds for anxiety and depression three years ago and, too timid to find a new doctor to write a prescription, I'm now stuck with watered-down over-the-counter crap. I don't pass out in gutters or bus stations or the beds of dubious women; I always manage to straighten my sheets and fluff my pillow, maybe even read a bit before losing consciousness.

Hemingway, now there was a guy who had demons—manly, strapping demons. Fitzgerald, he sure had his; so did Faulkner. Faulkner's demons could eat my demons' lunches any day of the week. But I digress.

Think, Muggins, think! "Write what you know"—that's the first thing they teach you.

Yes, an internal voice chides back, *that's just the problem*, to which I say, Huh?, to which the voice replies:

For heaven's sake, you've published two memoirs already, and you're not even running for president. Obviously, you've already scraped the bottom of the barrel, write-what-you-know-wise.

"Point taken," I note, falling all too easily into this internal ping-pong match yet again. "To be sure, I've wrung the old personal-narrative teat pretty much dry. But darn it, there must be something else I know—something I could bring a rare wealth of wisdom and experience to."

What about…wussitude?

"Say what?"

Wussitude—i.e., the quality of being a wussie, or the degree to which one is a wussie.

"Wh—why would that be an apt theme for me?"

Oh, come on—where do I start? You're terrified of being spoken to by strangers in public places, can't stand up to your own property manager—

"Okay, okay."

…Can't even look a charming and genial prostitute in the eye—

"Hey, that was just a walk."

Do I dare to eat a turkey-egg sandwich? Or a peach, for that matter?

"Hey, now! That's not funny. That's not funny and you know it!

Yes, yes. I know.

"Remember that time the in-laws served peaches?"

Oh, yeah.

"How was I supposed to know what to do with them? The Mugginses were never a fruit-eating family."

Hey, this is me you're talking to.

"Peaches are terrifying. People ought not to just thrust them at a fellow."

Relax. Take it easy. That was a long time ago. You're safe here. You've bolted the door. The peaches can't get at you.

"Hmm... Wussitude, eh? What's my way in?"

Think of some historical figures who were profound wussies. Hirohito leaps to mind.

"He does! Oh, he leaps! And Jefferson! Can't leave him out!"

So there's your foundation: biographical sketches of four or five prominent wussies.

"But...wouldn't that be, like... Like, hard? I'd have to do (gasp!)...research...wouldn't I?"

Some. But you could pad the whole business with the usual yakkity-yak about yourself. You've got some low-hanging fruit waiting for you wussie-anecdote-wise, my friend.

"Okay, now you're ticking me off. I suppose I have exhibited some wussie-like behavior of late. But you're suggesting a long history of it. Look, I was a normal kid growing up. Partied hard through six years of college. Had the nerve to move overseas to pursue a career. Courted and married a wonderful woman. Whatever's wrong with me now is surely just a phase."

Oh, come off it. Remember high school drama club?

"Ouch."

The cross-country drive with the three chicks back in Seventy-six?

"Ahh."

Cheryl Von Tunzelmann's leopard-spot bikini?

"A hit! A very palpable hit!"

I could go on like this all day. It's not like we're rushing off to scale any Himalayan peaks.

"You know, I begin to see it. I begin to see it. It just might work."

No shortage of material, I'm telling you.

"It could be a book, by cracky. A fully cohesive whole."

Trust me: Before you know it, you'll have three times the wordage you can use, and then it'll just be a matter of paring it down.

"Sculpting—that's what I call it."

The funnest part of the writing process!

"Where do I start?"

Get your wussie ass to Google, boy.

3. Wussie FAQ: Who's a Wussie? Hmm? Who's My Big Ussie-Wussie?

In the famous words of either Ronald Reagan or Howard Stern (I don't know about you, but I'm always getting them mixed up), let's make sure we know what we're talking about before we go off half-cocked.

Just what *is* a wussie? Who's in? Who's out? To get a feel for the concept I asked myself the following questions, thus making them by default the most Frequently Asked Questions about wussies.

Are chickenhawks wussies?

Well, I tell you. My quest to identify famous wussies from the past quickly got me stuck in semantic quicksand. It is almost a contradiction in terms, "famous wussie," since just about any man who has become famous got that way for doing something unwussie-like—indeed, more often than not for doing something downright bold and counterintuitive. Even Denis Thatcher.

Take the epithet *chickenhawk*, also known as "war wimp" in some quarters. The epithet has most often been applied to American politicians and pundits of the late twentieth and early twenty-first centuries who avoided participation in the Vietnam

War only to find themselves quite gung ho for shipping their children off to conflicts in the Middle East and Western Asia. And when I say "their children," the reader will understand that I am speaking in terms of the great metaphorical American family, not the alleged chickenhawk's actual offspring. For if a chickenhawk allowed his own flesh and blood to go off to war, it would enrage his ex-wives, of whom he lives in terror.

Rush Limbaugh, George Will, Dan Quayle, Newt Gingrich, Pat Buchanan, and much of the inner circle of the George W. Bush administration are the most commonly cited examples. Oh, and George W. Bush, too.

The thing that any true wussie notices, however, is that nowhere on this list can be found an individual who followed up his evasion of military service with an obscure career in a suitably wussie-like field: librarian, fast-food preparer, author of pseudonymously published books, etc.

No, every one of them chose a profession that placed him squarely in the arena, a career which regularly thrusts him into the searing glare of TV lights and pits him against passionate, motor-mouthed holders of opposing viewpoints in heated combat, if only of the verbal kind.

The pursuit of such careers—politician, pundit—in and of itself separates chickenhawks from authentic wussies, and the fact that such individuals regularly advocate sending young people into exactly the sort of armed conflict in hostile corners of the world that they themselves skulked away from is merely the frosting on the cake.

For at such bravura displays of duplicitous chutzpah the true wussie cringes with the proverbial shock and awe. The true wussie, having let his country down once, slinks away and is never heard from again on the subject of war—or on the subjects of kitchen wallpaper or the restructuring of the NBA playoffs, for that matter. He chooses a life that is secluded, subterranean, perhaps even Canadian, as seems only proper.

Can a woman be a wussie?

You would think so, since the very word *wussie* derives from a female's defining characteristic. And yet no famous examples spring to mind. Nor can I think of a single woman I have known, in Japan or back in the Satan—that I would characterize as a wussie.

I did once *call* several women the P word, though. I was teaching a compulsory freshman writing class at NU in Yokohama that year, a predominantly female group, and one day late in the term they were loudly bemoaning my piling on of homework when I snapped and just up and said, "Oh, what a bunch of [P-words]!" You'd be surprised how many Japanese young people are familiar with the anatomical but not the metaphorical meaning of that word.

I'm going to exercise my Constitutional right as a wussie to duck this question. Instead let me take this opportunity to note that it was a woman, Elizabeth Wurtzel, who wrote the book *Bitch: In Praise of Difficult Women*, which inspired both the title of this book and its barely coherent structure.

I remember taking great pride in buying that feminist screed soon after it came out—confident that it would raise my woefully low-riding consciousness on gender issues*—and then plodding through it in five-page increments while riding my exercise bike every night for the next six months. "Boy," I remember thinking, "feminists screeds sure are long, hard slogs." I developed a real admiration for those who ingest a steady diet of such material.

Six months on, the end of the book still not in sight, I went on line to see what other, speedier readers had made of it, and found out that no one, not even other feminists, had been able to make heads or tails of it. Even among avid Wurtzelites, I gather, *Bitch* is remembered as "that book Elizabeth wrote while she was out of

---

* Well, truth be told, the book's famous cover photo of a topless Elizabeth Wurtzel cheerfully flipping off readers may have had something to do with it, too. Now there, I thought at the time, is an author who knows how to move books.

her mind." I pressed on and finished it anyway, and let me tell you, whatever else Elizabeth Wurtzel may be, she's no wussie.

What about, like, a gay guy?

Glad you asked.

I grew up in a time and place where wussitude, homosexuality, and effeminacy were all lumped together as the same "disease." Or maybe one of them was the disease and the other two were symptoms. The whole thing was actually pretty complicated, rather like the early Christians' difficulties in unraveling the nature of the Holy Trinity.

I don't think the manly men of pre-disco Mortonville, Illinois ever felt the need to convene a Council of Nicaea to hammer the issue out, though. Their bottom line was simple: if a boy demonstrated any one of these traits, it meant that he surely possessed all three, and was to be razzed accordingly for the rest of his unnatural life.

By the time I was twelve I had acquired some sense of what this whole homosexuality thing amounted to in terms of the responsibilities of membership. What I was still sketchy on was how one got in in the first place. My assumption was that all boys started out heterosexual and that only those who failed to nail any chicks were then forced into gayness, in sort of the same way that failed journalists nowadays become bloggers.

It was therefore this threat of relegation to the less prestigious Homo Division that motivated me to start approaching girls at that age more than any actual attraction. I'd already been through this sort of thing a few years earlier with Little League.

Every Mortonville boy—even Chet Chudswell—aspired to make one of the six Little League teams. Those who failed the tryout, as I did, ended up in the so called Minor League, where it was common knowledge that they had to play any kid who showed up. Two long years of uniform-less, batting-tee-hitting humiliation, our games dumped to Saturday mornings with no live announcer to call us to the batter's box… Even parents begging off the obligation to attend… I would *not* allow that to happen again.

If it was to take me an inordinately long time to raise my consciousness—to cast off the gayness-equals-minor-league mindset and to parse the fallacious lumping together of gayness with feyness and wussitude—I blame the aforementioned Chet Chudswell. He grew up two blocks from me and was a colossal wussie who was also extremely effeminate. And as soon as he worked up the nerve to sashay his shirttail-tying, midriff-baring self into the back seat of Cliff Vanderhoven's rusted-out Chevy at the drive-in, he nailed the trifecta by proving to be enthusiastically homosexual as well.

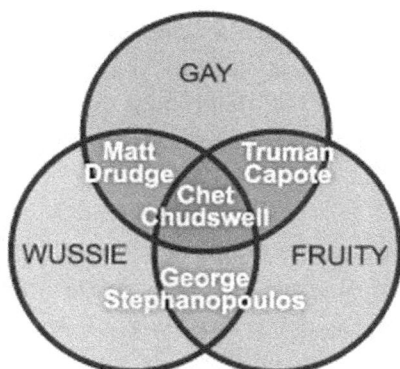

Figure 2: The limited overlap among wussie, fruity, and gay spheres.

It took years of unwilling contact with the world at large and the great variety of people in it for me to finally overturn the Chudswell Doctrine and figure out that wussitude, homosexuality, and effeminacy didn't always go hand in hand. Sure, an individual like Chet could come along and be all three things, but such a case was no more remarkable than someone happening to be, say, left-handed AND tri-nippled AND an Ice Dancing with the Stars contestant. Well, actually the Chudswell case was a bit less remarkable than that particular amalgamation. But presumably one gets the drift.

It was the choice to get out of Mortonville and live most of my adult life in Japan that proved critical to this consciousness raising. Gay Western expats are everywhere in Japan; you can't chuck a ninja star around Yokohama without braining one or two. I couldn't have mustered a wedding party without them. And the vast majority of them are neither wussies nor girlymen. And in my experience, when a gay Western expat happens to be one of those things, he is never the other.

What would Jesus do? Would he wuss out?

Jesus famously preached that the wussies would inherit the earth. Yes, true, the Bible doesn't actually say *wussies*, but raise your hand if you know the Aramaic word for *meek* in all of its nuances.

Was Jesus himself a wussie, then? All I know about the man is what I read in the papers, and the picture I'm getting is that of an individual who:

✓ goes toe to toe in debate with creepy grownups while still an adolescent

✓ feels at ease speaking in front of large crowds, even providing bountiful refreshments

✓ handles hecklers as tartly as Kathy Griffin

✓ never backs away from a face-off with Satan or his minions

✓ without a word, inspires a hot chick to slather perfume on His feet

✓   can start a table-turning ruckus in a public place in broad daylight without benefit of moonshine

✓   whines only briefly while being perforated with spikes and left to die

Who knows—maybe he was a colossal wussie who simply had a superb agent. He grew up in a Jewish neighborhood, after all. Still, my money's on *No* to the Jesus-as-wussie question.

The apostles, however, are quite another matter. Jesus may not have been a wussie himself, but he sure as heck was a fisher of wussies. Like a first-century version of a Hollywood studio mogul, he set about grabbing every suggestible lackey and butt-boy he could lay his hands on and giving them all fancy executive titles in his enterprise. Not until the formation of the Washington Generals basketball team in 1950 would the world see another twelve-pack of gullible, linguini-spined polliwogs comparable to this sorry assortment of fishnet-abandoning, thunderstorm-fearing, facedown -falling, three-time-friend-denying, garden-snoozing, crucifixion-no-showing, lot-casting, ghost-doubting ninnies.

Small wonder Jesus wept.

Is it inherently wussie-ish to write under an assumed name?

You bet it is. I'm rather glad you brought this up, as the whole pseudonym thing is a question I've wrangled with more and more of late. After two books written as Josh Muggins, an old friend advised me that it was time to come clean and show my real face this time out.

The urge to do so grows especially strong when a positive review of my work pops up on line, after which I strut around the next day feeling like Clark Kent: a disguised powerhouse waiting for any opportunity to fling off my glasses and peel off my shirt and magically ungrease my hair. Then there are the bad reviews, which make me feel rather like the Unabomber, more than happy to remain holed up in my cabin, tinkering and mumbling amid a funky stew of my own gases.

While this internal debate was raging one day, I stumbled upon the following story about a charming young film star of our era on a website called OMG.

LINDSAY LOHAN HAS A NEW MALE 'FRIEND'
February 1, 2008, 12:30 pm PST
Associated Press

WATERVILLE, Maine - A singer-songwriter from Maine who's filming a reality show with Lindsay Lohan is getting his 15 minutes of fame, and then some.

Jeremy Greene, a Waterville native, says he's being hounded by press calls after Life & Style magazine reported that Lohan referred to Greene as her "new boyfriend."

"It's good and it's bad," Greene told the Morning Sentinel newspaper. "It's like the gift and the curse."

The 25-year-old Greene, who was seen with Lohan in New York, received several text messages from her while being interviewed by the paper. He avoided questions on whether he and Lohan are dating -- "we're just friends" -- and says people will have to watch the show to see if there are any sparks.

Lohan's mother, Dina, contacted Greene last fall, he said. They did some initial shootings for the show and he and the Lohan family hit it off.

For the reality show, Greene and the Lohan family will live on the top floor of the Palms Casino Hotel in Las Vegas, where there's a swimming pool and a full music recording studio, among other things.

As for the media attention, it kicked into high gear on Monday when Greene was seen with Lohan at the Four Seasons Hotel in New York City.

Will he ever bring Lindsay to Maine?

"I told her we have good lobster," he said. "You never know."

For the benefit of post-2015 readers:

During the first decade of the millennium—the PlayStation 2 years, if that helps—Lindsay Lohan won acclaim and a certain amount of notoriety as a talented, feisty young actress with an irrepressible zest for life. I became aware of her during her teen years when her marvelously mature comic performance in an early project, *Freaky Friday*, brightened a few hours of a long trans-Pacific flight. Later, after her blossoming into young womanhood (actually more of an overnight gamma-ray mutation into young womanhood), I began to feel a closer connection to her, one tinged with the type of paternalistic concern that the real Lohan *père* appeared to have long since abdicated.

The late Ms. Lohan navigated the world under her real name in those tempestuous times, despite the embarrassment many of her father's antics surely brought on her, and her courage under fire shames us pseudonym-using wussies. Consider the reader comments below, which I managed to preserve from the same site before they dissipated into the ether. All ten of the comments (numbers 69 to 78 in a seemingly endless run) were uploaded in a space of three minutes in response to the benign gossip item printed above.

"Id-Hit-It-And-Run" leads off with a heartfelt "Linday I hope the next celeberity death is you."

"Amanda" notes: "wow, i just wasted a minute of sleep reading this garbage."

"harold h" inquires: "Just who hasn't she screwed? My guess, its only a handfull of Iranians. ...she's certainly screwed the entire male population of North America. . .can't really say she's any good, either…"

"mexi0501" chimes in to remind everyone that "this is lame," to which mike w astutely retorts, "ummmmm, if ur postin then obviously u read it too."

"crazy" wants the rest of humanity to be aware that "id do her," a notion quickly seconded by "D Bag": "She's still hawt. nyuk nyuk."

"Sarah," apparently distracted by a concurrent discussion taking place offstage, notes, "Hey KIM- First off you little smart a@!, I don't have a drug addiction problem do you? Kind of sounds like it if you are sticking up for her. Do I know what an 8 ball is? Sure do honey. Have I ever snorted one, ran my car in to a tree? Ended up in REHAB? Been nicknamed 'fire crotch' because I 'F' anything that walks by me. NOPE, To smart"…

…to which "crazy," perhaps unsure as to whether or not all present have digested his earlier views, avers that "I dont care id put it in her butt. lol."

It falls to "Rocket" to tie up the disparate threads of this haphazard collaboration, and he rises to the occasion with "i can't believe you all waste time on this crap."

At the end of each "posting" sits a link labeled "Report abuse," which begs the question: Couldn't I just report what's *not*? But to sum up: The most benign mention imaginable of Lindsay Lohan in early 2008 could generate more nasty vitriol in the space of three minutes than one of my whole books could in half a year.

It is unclear whether or not Lindsay herself read the above comments. If so, she nobly refrained from responding to them, unless her decision to sit for her first authorized nude photos later that same month constituted a response. If so, one could hardly hope for a more appropriate rebuke to her spelling- and capitalization-challenged detractors. *In your faces, Id-Hit-It-And-Run and harry h! I have a thick skin, and here it is!*

Still, one has to take the long view here. Lindsay may have won this round but not the war. Nefarious trolls would continue to denounce her and still are doing so even as I type these words, and she can't just keep playing the nude-photo-shoot card in retaliation every time. Even such formidable charms as Lindsay's are bound to bring diminishing returns over time.

And even if she herself is thick-skinned enough to bear it all, what about the impact on Lohans yet unborn? They can't all hide out in Maine gorging on that good lobster forever. Early in the 22nd century, will some fourth-generation Lohan put out the telepathic equivalent of a Facebook page, only to be besieged by the petty, undigested, quasi-English brain farts of fourth-generation harolds and Sarahs?

I think I'll keep on cowering behind "Josh Muggins" for a while yet, if it's all the same to you.

Who else is a wussie, then?

Google was, of course, invented for precisely this purpose, so that's where I began my research back in Waikiki.

A search for "famous [P-word]" brought up nothing but porn sites, sites devoted to pop starlets, and the odd site for cat-lovers. This was worse than fruitless in that it dragged me off track for several hours—kitten-video sucker that I am.

Finally I searched for "...is a wussie," then "...are wussies," after which I repeated both searches substituting in the P-word.

So here is a snapshot of whom the wired world regarded as wussies as of September 20, 2007:

Socrates
Corey Feldman
Don Imus

Miyata (martial arts fighter)
Randy Moss
"Christopher"
Ben Ferguson
Brent Bozell
America
Sean Penn
Superman
"Gordon"
"Fire Tigah"
You
Vincent Pastore
He
"Dave"
Toyota
"Bill"
Vodkarella
50 Cent
I
"Andrew"
Jon Heder
Ben Silverman
"Richard" (for not going through with the rape)
Allah
Perez Hilton
Kobe Bryant
Tank Levy
"Keanes"
Jimmy Carter
Dean Baquet
Heather Mills
Veronica Jett's husband
Howard Stern
"Spoon"
Ted Nugent

"BrendO"

A cop who didn't draw his weapon even though this one guy tried to run over him

4. *Profiles in Wussitude, Vol. 1*

A Wuss of Biblical Proportions

All right. We now have a serviceable concept of our twenty-first century wussie. All well and good, but one can never attain full self-knowledge without uncovering one's roots. Thus, one final question cries out to be addressed: Who was the first wussie?

There looms one enormous obstacle to coping with this

question, of course, and that obstacle is that no one cares. I've got to admit that I'm not too spellbound by the matter myself, but a search for the *Ur*-wussie looks like the easiest way for me to make my daily word quote in time to mentally undress Rachael Ray and whoever her guest might be. So let's get started.

By rights, our search ought to begin in the ravines of Hadar, northern Ethiopia, some 3.2 million years ago, where we might expect to see a three-and-a-half-foot, sixty-pound proto-hominid named Lucy slapping around her fifteen-year-old son—call him Skip—one chilly morning for clinging to her withered dugs when he ought to be joining his dozen-odd surviving siblings in yet another invigorating session of hunter-gathering out on the damp and open savannah.

In his later years, the stubbornly dug-clinging Skip would bear witness to those two great inventions of primitive man, controlled fire and the wheel, and instinctively recoil in fear at both of them. Subsequently, he would retreat from the very sight of the sun (a flaming wheel) into a dark cave, never to be seen again.

Our search indeed *ought* to begin there, but taking that route is likely to anger Creationists, who as a rule cut much more fearful figures when poked with a stick than do paleoanthropologists. Another point in favor of the Creationist approach to tracing humanity's wussie roots is the existence of a nifty paper trail in the form of the Bible. So let's start there.

—□—

It is tempting, then—not to mention lazy—to seize upon Adam as the first wussie. Consider his résumé: There's his ill-advised pose for the ceiling of the Sistine Chapel, for starters, in which the ripped and shaved, gay-porn-ready Adam gives God the dead-fish handshake. Any publicist worth her salt would have nixed that pose, or at least sued the artist after the fact to milk more headlines out of it.

Problem with Adam is that there is no basis for comparison.

Adam sets the baseline by which the virility of all subsequent males is to be measured. And if it seems that he sets the standard pretty low, well, consider that he is fated to spend most of his public life alone with God and Eve, both of whom can be pretty controlling.

Indeed, Adam is easily browbeaten by his soulmate into breaking practically the only rule imposed on him, after which he flees and tries to hide from God. Which works about as well as you might suppose it would. "Where art thou?" yells God, as if He doesn't know. Then He stages an intervention at which He chews everybody out in turn: the serpent, Eve, and finally Adam:

Because thou hast hearkened unto the voice of thy wife, and hast eaten of the tree…cursed is the ground for thy sake; in sorrow shalt thou eat of it all the days of thy life; thorns also and thistles shall it bring forth to thee; and thou shalt eat the herb of the field: in the sweat of thy face shalt thou eat bread, till thou return unto the ground.

So Adam skulks off, resigned to centuries of sweaty-faced bread-eating in the wilderness.* God no longer returns his calls and the serpent never shows any interest in him, Eve being so much more intriguing, so he figures the only way he'll ever enjoy convivial male companionship is to start churning out his own convivial male companions.

And we all know how well that little Family Circus would turn out. Which brings us to the second candidate for the title of first wussie: Abel.

—□—

---

* It doesn't really sound that awful out of context: more like a minor inconvenience. But imagine hearing *directly from God* that you have to eat bread with a sweaty face from now on. Wouldn't that put a different, more mortifying spin on just about any seemingly petty indignity? "With thy zipper half open shalt thou present thy slideshows." "On thy most innocent strolls shalt thou be accosted by comely streetwalkers." Etc.

Abel, you'll recall, was the first person who managed to annoy someone else into killing him, that someone being his brother, Cain.

These two were the prototypes for the lads in the classic *Highlights* cartoons, Cain being the irrepressible wildass and Abel the insufferable goody-goody: Goofus runs with the jawbone of an ass pointed up; Gallant runs with the jawbone pointed down. Goofus offers a crappy little sacrifice that likes God not; Gallant prepares *his* sacrifice carefully and pleases God. Goofus lures Gallant to a remote field to coldcock him; Gallant dies. Goofus lips off to God: "Am I my brother's keeper?"; Gallant's blood politely cries out to God from the ground. Needless to say, Goofus/Cain is the more compelling character here. People don't seem to remember much about Abel—a fact that boosts his candidature as First Wussie.

But mere obscurity does not a wussie make. While the Bible gives only the tersest account of Abel's demise, the consensus among artists who have depicted the scene—Rubens, Tintoretto Manfredi, Negretti—makes one thing clear: Abel most likely fought back. He did not go gentle into that good night. He did not turn the other cheek. One anonymous master envisions Abel fighting the good fight even as the unsportsmanlike Cain, getting his full Goofus on, knees his brother in his bare-naked nuts.

And it is this capacity for fierce resistance that paints Abel (quite literally) in a very different light from the figure who emerges as the brightest candidate for Western Civ's true *Ur*-wussie: Isaac.

—◻—

Like Abel before him, Isaac is best remembered as a hapless victim of domestic violence. The critical differences are these:

(1) Isaac's tormenter is not his brother, but his father, and

(2) Isaac doesn't die—at least, not just yet.

For those who missed Sunday school that week, here are the

particulars:

When Isaac was eight days old his father, Abraham, cut off his foreskin, thereupon launching a religious custom as well as a zany family tradition in which Dad would periodically brandish knives over a stunned and helpless Isaac. And people say the Osbournes are excessively goth.

The most notorious of these episodes began when God, in one of His moods, ordered Abraham to take his son out somewhere nice, spend some quality time with the boy, and then slaughter him. So Abraham led Isaac out to Mount Moriah and had the lad gather up sticks while he once again got out his trusty old blade.

In the Bible, Abraham remains the central character throughout this melodrama. We're invited to share his suffering over this awful dilemma: to kill his only remaining son, or to disobey God. The narrator never pauses to consider how the whole episode might have affected Isaac. Abraham at least had the considerable advantage of direct communication with God. Isaac hears nothing from On High. Isaac gets bupkis. Having spent so much time communicating all the details of the plan to Abraham, God could have troubled Himself to let Isaac in on the deal, you would think, even if only in the form of some sort of hastily tapped-out heavenly tweet:

pa wll kll u 2day ok? ☺

But no: God and Abraham decide to leave Isaac out of the loop on this one.

So at some point in the course of the day, Dad explains his purpose to Isaac. The Bible once again shortchanges us here. We don't know quite how Abraham put it, but it must have been good. By all accounts, the youngster allows himself to be bound to a rock without a peep.

That's how Isaac is portrayed in much of the artwork of this famous scene: as a youngster—a prepubescent boy or perhaps a young teen. The Bible doesn't assign him an age, but scholars now place him at the time of the incident somewhere in the twenty-five to thirty-seven range.

Which sort of alters one's perspective on the whole scenario, no? When I was, say, eight, if my father had sat me down one Saturday morning and told me that, darn the luck, I would have to be taken out and tied to a rock and stabbed to death instead of going to the Cub Scout Swim, I, too, might have played along with him in my wide-eyed innocence.

When I was twenty-five to thirty-seven, on the other hand, I'd like to think that I would have been much less amenable to this proposal. More to the point, by the time I got to be that age, my father was fifty-eight to seventy.

As he was a gentle and funny man who loved me unconditionally, we were fated never to test the issue of whether or not he could have bound me to a rock against my will during that period of our lives—or any other period, for that matter. In retrospect, though, I'd like to think that I could have eluded the clutches a man of that age and, for good measure, tied *his* crazy white ass to a rock until proper authorities could be summoned. Throw in the nugget that Abraham was one hundred years old *when Isaac was born*, and suddenly the full scope of Isaac's magnificent wussitude comes into view.

While artists flubbed Isaac's age, the expression on Isaac's face in a good many of the more popular depictions—the Laurent de la Hyre painting reprinted above for one, the Rembrandt rendition for another—look about right given the circumstances. Abraham consistently appears irked and distracted by the intrusion of the angel bearing God's stay of execution. "Hang on—this'll only take a second," one can imagine him saying, and then the angel is, like, "No, seriously, dude—you don't have to go through with it," to which Abraham is all, "Dad blast it, get your wings out of my face! Can't you see I've got a throat to slit here?" with Isaac having to listen to all this while trying to suck in some air between his father's fingers.

Five Fun Facts About Isaac

✓ His name means "may God laugh," because his mother Sarah thought that her pregnancy so late in life was a practical joke by the Big Fellow.

✓ Isaac was Abraham's first legitimate son but he had an older half-brother, Ishmael, born of Abraham's favorite side-dish, Hagar. Ishmael was fated to be written out of the Bible story when Abraham had him and his mother run out of camp. Hagar went on to inspire a perennially mediocre comic strip.

✓ Isaac was the only patriarch who never left Canaan. Not that he didn't try. Canaan being a place where people had this unfortunate tendency to raise knives over him, he quite naturally made a break for it once. But God made him stay put.

✓ When the sacrifice of Isaac was averted, angels were said to have cried tears of joy which fell upon his face. Some believe that Isaac's blindness in old age was a latent effect of these tears, proving the adage that you can't win for losing sometimes.

✓ Isaac is listed among the prophets of Islam in the Koran, making it a really bad idea for a wussie like me to make light of him in print.

Isaac's face in these works is the face of a third-string quarterback sent in for the first time all season with the task of protecting a slim lead in the fourth quarter of the Super Bowl. And in that face, anyone can find a brother, a colleague, a cafeteria lunchmate, a fellow porn-site commenter. An overmatched high school drama coach. Himself.

All of which would be humiliating enough had Dad followed through and ended his misery right then and there, but no. Isaac is to survive and grow old and follow his father into the Old Testament patriarch business. But at the end of a very long career, all anyone will remember him for is that one oft-depicted father-son outing.

Imagine that every photo published in every yearbook of your high school career depicted the single most humiliating episode of your four-year tenure there—having your gym shorts pulled down in front of the cheerleading squad, say, or vomiting all over your pretty lab partner as she smartly dissects a frog. The snapshots may differ slightly in angle and tint, but it's nonetheless the same unbearable scene, year after year, over and over and over again. This gives you a taste of what it means to be Isaac.

—◻—

Having survived that ordeal without benefit of therapy, Isaac has to get on with his life. He is obliged to set about finding a mate to help him grind out the next round of patriarchs, but this is no easy task when you're already forty and you never get out of your hometown and you've got aging parents to deal with, at least one of whom is still frisky and overdue to turn on you again. Left to his own devices, Isaac, like any other true wuss, is never going to get laid.

Here, Abraham steps in and finds his son a nice mail-order bride—rather an extraordinary office for a father, but their history being what it is, probably the least he can do. Isaac finds Rebekah a fine woman—not that he has any basis for comparison, but he's honestly nuts for the girl. To no one's surprise, though, it will take him twenty years to impregnate her.

Finally Rebekah bears twins, Jacob and Esau. The former, who is favored by Rebekah, grows up to be a patriarch. The latter, who is favored by Isaac, grows up to be a wussie—and a wussie with a serious back-hair problem at that.

Strictly speaking, we should call Esau "the former" as he was the first of the twins out of the chute, and primogeniture holds sway in that time and place. But later on Jacob pulls a fast one on his superannuated, blind father, putting on a hairy coat in order to be mistaken for the shaggy Esau and then receiving his father's blessing, which, under the slipshod legal code of the day, makes *him* the primary heir and leaves Esau out in the cold with only his remarkably hairy body for comfort.

Jacob would use this deception as a springboard to a Hall of Fame career as an Old Testament patriarch, ending up in practically the same class as his grandfather, Abraham. Jacob chats with God, is allowed to see the stairway to heaven long before Jimmy Page, wrestles an angel to a draw, and fathers more sons with more women than an NBA shooting guard. Meanwhile, Isaac stays home and knits socks or something.

Indeed, as Old Testament patriarchs go, Isaac would end up in that awkward Jan Brady category of history's middling figures bookended by titans. In effect, he was John Adams to their Washington and Jefferson, George Lazenby to their Connery and Moore, the cocoon to their caterpillar and butterfly, Joe Besser to their Curly and Shemp, Thanksgiving to their Halloween and Christmas. Hua Guofeng to their Mao and Deng. Frankincense to their gold and myrrh. Apollo 12 to their 11 and 13. Depression to their Anger and Acceptance. All right, then. No need to beat a dead horse about it.

Isaac would die the classic wussie's death of natural causes abetted by embarrassment at the tender age of one hundred and eighty. He was buried in the Tomb of the Patriarchs, probably because there was no Tomb of the Wussies. He is still remembered today by children forced or bribed to memorize Bible passages.

Patriarchal standings as measured by prominent namesakes*

Though a bit heavy on science geeks and Scientologists, the list of namesakes of Isaac trumps those of his father and son.

Notable Isaacs	Newton, Asimov, Hayes, Hanson, Mirazhi, Bashevis Singer
Notable Abrahams	Lincoln, ("Bram") Stoker, Zapruder, Vigoda
Notable Jacobs	Astor, Gyllenhaal, Delhomme, Dylan, demigod on *Lost*

* Source: A 45-second Google search

---

5. The Wussie/Wookiee Test

These two male archetypes are often confused, as both make for high-maintenance boyfriends. To ascertain which category that special fellow in your life falls into, check all that apply.

My boyfriend...

_____ 1. Is handy with engines

_____ 2. Was featured in a legendary holiday TV special

_____ 3. Wails uncontrollably at the sight of freeze-dried carcasses of longtime companions

_____ 4. Presents with poor personal hygiene, especially hair care

_____ 5. Wallops storm troopers fearlessly with mammoth paws

_____ 6. Thinks about cauliflower to stave off premature ejaculation

_____ 7. Can melt platinum with his urine

_____ 8. Blames himself when stoned teenage barista concocts wrong flavored frappuccino

_____ 9. Whimpers when spayed

_____ 10. Easily grasps the flaws in Marcusean attacks on Satrean existentialism, but is too shy to say anything about them

Scoring: Taking this quiz indicates obsessive-compulsive disorder.

6. Rolling Fella

If you have a wussie friend who has confessed to a long unslaked need to be serviced by a lifeless, eyeless, parboiled infant—or, for that matter, a *mustachioed* lifeless, eyeless, parboiled infant—I know just the stocking stuffer for him: the "Rolling Fella Bomba," available now in fine adult goods stores near you. Or at least, near me.

I remember the first time I held this twelve-ounce polyurethane bundle of joy in my arms. It smiled up at me; then frowned; then smiled again; then frowned again, the constantly shifting mood on its iridescent pink features provoked by the enormous spear-like tongue lolling around between its cheeks as if trying to dislodge a particularly stubborn clump of peanut butter.

I knew my life would never be the same again as I fiddled with the dial on the attached battery-powered control. The little gizmo seemed to wink at me, and no doubt actually would have, had it only had eyes. In addition to the aforementioned tongue, it came with lips (unadorned on the version I chose; mustachioed on another), a pert little nose, and a cherubic chin and cheeks. *Whirrrrr*, it cooed faintly during the obligatory in-store demonstration: *Whirr, whirr.*

Its squishy baby-sized half-face flowed necklessly into a rubbery, cylindrical, foot-long body, giving the device the overall form of either the title character of *Alien* in full jaw-extension mode, or the logo of the 2007 New England Patriots chopped flat just below the three-corner hat.

Between those two analogs (an acid-blooded killing machine, a cold-blooded scoring machine) I had no preference. In truth, it quickly became apparent that the presence of the miniature facial features added nothing to the product's appeal—you'd not wish to make eye contact with the thing even if it had eyes—and that they existed only to assure maximum embarrassment to the owner in case of the device's discovery by others.

Then again, only the mustachioed version could guarantee truly *maximum* embarrassment. Still, the bare-lipped version I purchased would prove mortifying enough if discovered by, say, Mrs. Muggins. Or the guy who checks the smoke detectors. Or any of the other seven billion inhabitants of the planet.

—▫—

Perhaps the reason for the face is to cement the item's status as a gag gift, though this would seem to depend on which definition of *gag* is intended. You see, the box plainly states (in Japanese), "This is a gag gift. The manufacturer bears no responsibility for instances of its use for other purposes."

The copy on the box also explains the name. The Rolling Fella Bomba is not, as the ignorant might suppose, an instrument for bombing fellas. *Fella* in this case is short for fellatio. The bombing part, however, is quite sincere: The "o" in the word *Bomba* takes the shape of a cartoon bomb with a burning fuse. No doubt this bomb is a metaphor for the explosive laughter you and your friend will share when he opens this hilarious eighty-dollar gag gift, batteries included.

Above the item's name on the front side of the box is a picture of a bored Japanese woman hiking up her skirt and squatting on a cylindrical object obscured by a cartoon thought-bubble. Evidently the contents of the bubble express the woman's thoughts, though those thoughts appear to be emanating from inside her skirt rather than from that traditional seat of reason, the head. If you offered a penny for those thoughts, you would reap this improbable windfall:

The whole mouth moves in a circular motion when the switch is on, while the tongue rolls around! You can heighten your pleasure by applying the lubricant!

On a side of the box, there is another picture of the same woman, this time with the obscured cylinder filling her mouth. She again looks bored and vaguely irritated. * The script running alongside the woman's head reads, "Please excuse me for making you feel too good," a sentiment that her expression coats with sarcasm. Other cover copy includes: "Explosive spermifying!" "Intense fella-play!" and perhaps the easiest question ever addressed to male consumers in the history of ad copy: "Do you like being fellated?"

The "Intense fella-play!" message is reiterated on the back of the box, along with a website for gag-gift aficionados who have further questions, and in fine print:

Please recycle after use.

On the remaining side of the box, there are four small close-ups of the same overtaxed lady taken from slightly different angles with different percentages of the obscured cylinder in her mouth. Then there are these instructions:

Apply the lubricant and then enter through the mouth.† Turn on the switch, and the whole mouth begins moving in a circular motion! At the same

---

* This, it should be noted, actually represents a stride of sorts in the ethics of Japanese pornographers. For decades they delighted in humiliating and hurting Japanese women. Now they seem content merely to annoy them.
† Duh.

time, the tongue also moves in circles, too, licking your honorable chinchin. The intensity of the movement can be adjusted by manipulating the control, so that you can select the speed that pleasures you best! Recommended for fella maniacs! 120% satisfaction!

At my adult goods store in the Shinjuku district of Tokyo, the Rolling Fella Bomba has earned the coveted "Owner's Recommended Product!" tag made of pink construction paper and magic markers of various cheery colors.

They have two Rolling Fella Bombas in stock: One for 7,200 yen and one for 8,200 yen. I wonder if the markdown is due to some damage. No, the clerk assures me, the two are the same in every respect. The 7,200-yen tag is a mistake, though he'll let me have it for that—but I'm suspicious. I wonder if the clerk has actually removed this item from the box and tried it out on himself. Because that's what I'd do if I found myself working in an adult goods store. I'd try out every item that I'm anatomically qualified for, then put them back in their plastic wrap and boxes and sell them—but with a slight markdown to assuage my guilt.

—◻—

Nobody asked me, but here is my capsule review of the Rolling Fella Bomba.

As a gag gift, it was an unqualified washout. Perhaps it would have been funnier had I given it to someone other than myself. Speaking as the recipient, a whole raft of emotions, including that venerable couple Fear and Loathing, oozed over me in the course of perusing and then using this item, but sidesplitting mirth was conspicuously AWOL from that lineup.

As an instrument of explosive spermifying, on the other hand, I must say that I found it insuperable. I would proudly deliver a televised commercial endorsement of this fine product, complete with live demonstration, for no compensation beyond the costs of extensive plastic surgery, permanent relocation and three forged passports.

Really, the only thing preventing me from giving this product the coveted five-star rating is the appearance. It is impossible to use the Fella Bomba, or to look at it, or even to tacitly acknowledge its existence in my apartment without contemplating the risk of its discovery by visitors. Let's face it, one is not going to be able to pass the nose-lips-and-tongue-having little devil off as a neck massager or some such benign thing, as women's sex toys once were and perhaps still are in Mormon households. Nothing could be more demeaning to a card-carrying wuss than to die with a Fella Bomba in the bottom of his t-shirt drawer.

Actually, that's not true. Indeed, death would be the most welcome of all possible preludes to the discovery of the Fella Bomba. The most demeaning outcome would be to end up alive but too incapacitated to prevent its discovery. Many a time this nightmare scenario has seized on my mind:

At the small apartment near the university where I reside alone while school is in session, I suffer a seizure and am barely able to summon paramedics in time. Mrs. Muggins then arrives from our primary home in the provinces to be at my bedside when I regain consciousness in the hospital, whereupon this conversation—if the term applies—would ensue:

Me: Oh, hi. Thanks for coming up here to be at my bedside.

Mrs. Muggins: ...

Me: I see you've brought a change of clothes for me.

Mrs. Muggins: ...

Me: Guess that means you've been in the t-shirt drawer, eh?

Mrs. Muggins: …

Me: Yes, yes. I can see that you have, then.

Mrs. Muggins: …

Me: Well. Well, well, well…

Mrs. Muggins: …

Me: It was a gag gift! I swear it!

Mrs. Muggins: …

Me: Oh, all right. It wasn't a gag gift. I bought it for myself! I admit it! A man has needs, Michiko! What do you want me to do? Don't answer that!

Mrs. Muggins: …

Me: Trust me, it could have been worse. At least I threw the box away.

However, in the three-way race to oblivion, it turned out that the Rolling Fella Bomba would be the first to succumb, leaving it to Mrs. Muggins and me to vie for place and show.

Yes, there came that day when my Rolling Fella Bomba's perky *Whirrrrr!* became a weary and spasmodic *whirrRrrrrRRRRrrrrr RRRR….rrrr…RRR…rrr…* Fresh batteries were no help at all. The old thing had taken hundreds of hits and soapy rinsings without complaint since I had brought it home. It was around ninety-five in people years, and let's face it, nobody wants to explosively spermify into something that old in people years. *Whir, whirrr*, it murmured, like the Little Sex Toy that Could. I said, take a rest, old friend. You've done enough.

—◻—

I only briefly considered bringing it back to the shop as per recycling instructions. Perhaps there really is some sort of adult-goods UNICEF that collects these things and redistributes them to poor, starving perverts in godforsaken lands, but I doubt it. Even if there were, who would adopt a whirring, arthritic-tongued Fella Bomba? They say beggars can't be choosers, but come on.

But if recycling is out, what *do* I do with the…well, with the corpse? There is more to be considered here than my dignity, after all. There is the matter of doing the right thing by…by *it*.

Consider that even the earliest humans invested their favorite objects and possessions with animistic spirits and parted with them only under duress. The ancients would insist on being buried with their most beloved things. We're talking about items like pipes or bowls. If Natural Man could get so worked up over crockery, how on earth would he have coped with the demise of a household appliance with soft humanoid features that had been very much animate in its prime (with fresh batteries), a thing that had provoked him to dozens of the most glorious hands-free orgasms of his entire ejaculatory career? If you put it in that light, then taking the trouble to push the Fella Bomba out to sea on a flaming Viking ship would not seem excessive in the least.

All this dithering was getting me nowhere. I had no Viking ship, and anyway lacked access to a stretch of vacant beach where I could execute such an elaborate send-off. My alternatives came down to a simple few, unworthy of the Fella Bomba though they were:

Solution	Pluses	Minuses
(A) Put it out in the regular trash	Easily done	My apartment building has no dumpster, only a specified area at the curb of a public street with a vinyl net to protect the garbage from animals. It would be left sitting there in a semitransparent bag for all the neighbors to see until pick-up, and there's no guarantee that sanitary workers *would* pick it up after they had glimpsed it through the plastic. What the hell *was* it, anyway? Burnable? Non-burnable? Plastic container?
(B) Dump it in somebody else's trash	Lack of traceability	(1) Requires more nerve than I've got when sober. (2) Is evil.

(B) won out easily. After auditioning some likely locales, I settled on the Seven-Eleven halfway between my apartment and the local train station. First, I wrapped Fella Bomba in newspaper; then I laid it in a shoebox: basically the dead hamster treatment. Then, on a Sunday morning, my cowardice sufficiently dulled by a blinding hangover, I took Fella Bomba for its last ride.

Actually, this was also its first ride, seeing as (leaving out our trip home from the store) I had never taken it anywhere. That sudden realization made me very sad. *I never took it anywhere.*

At the Seven-Eleven, some high school girls were loitering near the recycling bins, unable to decide whether to eat their snacks on the spot or save them for later. I waited around the corner until they moved on. Taking a deep breath, I made my move. I stuffed the box into the burnables bin, but it came bouncing halfway out again because the bin was full. I wrangled with it for several long seconds, finally managing to stuff it inside the flap where it nestled atop other trash, just as I saw the clerk heading straight for me with a new garbage bag.

I staggered away, feeling his eyes burning holes in the back of my head as he opened up the burnables bin and—though I couldn't see this, somehow did see it—handled the shoebox with curiosity, shaking it, feeling the presence of some soft, pliant thing shifting around inside. I kept walking. *He didn't see my face,* I reminded myself. Which was odd, since I had seen his. I didn't know him, but he certainly fit the general description of a student at my school. Which meant he would recognize me, since all foreign teachers are celebrities, even if I didn't recognize him.

I dismissed these paranoid ravings from my mind until passing by the Seven-Eleven on my return from other errands near the train station. From a different angle now, I noticed something I'd missed earlier: the security camera pointed squarely at the recycling bins. And that's when I vowed to change jobs. And move house. And dip my fingertips in acid.*

Three days later I made the long trek up to Shinjuku to purchase a new Fella Bomba.

—◻—

By the time Rolling Fella Bomba II was on its last legs—last lips— whatever—I had grown less sentimental. Even while it was still delivering the goods, I found myself thinking, with only a pinch of guilt, that it would soon be time to move on, much the way one might watch the beloved old family dog wheezing her way up the steps and catch oneself visualizing the cute, frisky puppy that will soon succeed her with perhaps the same name.

I set up an internal committee within my subconscious to hammer out a disposal plan well in advance this time, one that

---

* Okay, I later thought better of the acid. But I really did change jobs and move house, and the Seven-Eleven Incident was by no means a non-factor in those decisions.

eschewed the danger of security cameras and student spies. A chap can't go around changing jobs and moving house every time he has a fleshy, eyeless, limp-tongued, iridescent corpse-like thing to get rid of, after all. Still, the committee's recommendation made me quail. It would require some of that scarce emolument, nerve, to put into action.

Inserting the sewing scissors into the mouth of the late Fella Bomba II, I snipped an incision down the side of the head where the right ear should have been, then kept snipping to the end of the shaft. I was then able to peel the soft tissue off the animating mechanism beneath. Then I snipped and snipped and snipped, determined not to leave any piece large enough for a meddlesome neighbor or sanitary worker to suppose ever to have been part of a face, all the while chewing on the not terribly surprising revelation that I would have made a lousy mobster.

Then I got drunk. The next morning, I took the burnable portion of the remains out to the trash-net; that afternoon, I took its replacement out of the box.

— ◻ —

On an impulse, I had purchased a completely different item this time. The picture on the box rather grabbed me. A rippingly handsome and jaunty young Caucasian model was reclining in an easy chair, naked, with the device encasing his member like a giant upside-down test tube.

Removed from the box for the obligatory in-store battery test, it gave a favorable if mystifying impression. There was no face, no waggling tongue. With luck, in the event of its discovery after my seizure, I might be able to persuade the discoverer that the thing was a new-fangled popcorn popper or some such.

Inside the larger plastic test tube was a smaller one, and in the space between the two tubes, two bracelets of shiny blue marbles or beads were suspended. The clerk flipped the switch on the control, causing the bracelets to slide rapidly up and down the shaft of the interior test tube. It sounded like a ball-bearing spill across a busy six-lane highway.

"Could you show me what it looks like running on Slow?" I shouted.

"This *is* Slow," replied the clerk, a small, feral lad who had seen it all. His mustache looked exactly like the one painted on the gay version of Rolling Fella Bomba.

I was trying to formulate the words "Sorry, but it seems a bit too much for me," after which I would snatch the last Fella Bomba off the shelf, but the words caught in my throat as the clerk telepathically flung the thought "I'm not going to remove all six of these C batteries and re-package this thing" at me. I got that message loud and clear. Maybe all those batteries boosted his signal.

"I guess I'll take it," I yelled, and sadly forked over the equivalent of a hundred dollars.

— ¤ —

My illicit affair with the non-Fella Bomba toy lasted all of 20 seconds. If compelled to say something positive about it, I guess I could offer this: The ad copy quite accurately made no claims that the device was in any way funny.

I honestly have forgotten the name under which the thing was marketed in Japan, but I would submit "the Penis Peeler" as my entry in a naming contest. I suppose it sounds like something the Popeil people might cheerfully and officiously demonstrate in an infomercial at two in the morning, or perhaps a new epithet for powerful women that sexists could adopt once they finally weary of "ballbreaker." *That Hillary Clinton,* they could say. *What a penis peeler!*

Hold on, I now recall another positive thing to say on behalf of the Penis Peeler: It was easy to throw away.

As of this writing, I'm on Fella Bomba VI and I've learned not to stray. And now that I've told you all this, please excuse me while I find a nice cozy rock to crawl under and die.

7. The Wussies of Shakespeare

and *Leave it to Beaver*

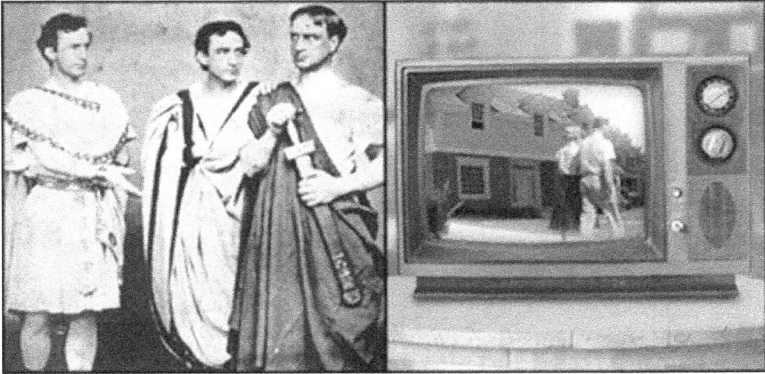

Two great fonts of wisdom have produced the lion's share of Western Civilization's wussie archetypes. Here, those sources are brought together for the first comprehensive overview. *

---

* I'm assured that the photograph on the right is the *Leave It To Beaver* house. What you should be seeing here is a picture of the *Leave It To Beaver* cast, which would better balance the left-hand picture of the nineteenth-century Booth brothers enacting *Julius Caesar.* Thing is, Getty Images owns the rights to *Leave It To Beaver* promotional photos, and do you know how much they expected me to pay them just to put one measly picture into this book? Five hundred twenty-seven dollars and forty-six

63

Character (Work)	Wuss Credentials	Signature Line
Falstaff (Henry IV)	Runs away in midst of a highway robbery in which he's the robber; plays dead on the battlefield; sucks up to young Prince Hal.	"I would 'twere bed-time, Hal, and all well."
Pistol (Henry IV, Henry V)	Is cowed even by Falstaff; a babbling Welshman makes him his bitch.	"Must I bite?"
The twin Dromios (The Comedy of Errors)	Are routinely beaten not only by their own masters but by each other's.	"But I pray, sir, *why* am I beaten?"
Richard II (Richard II)	Is deposed not by a bloodthirsty horde but by a garrulous committee; coup leader appropriates his horse just to rub it in; dies screaming in prison; full name of play in fifth quarto was "The Tragedie of the Foofie Wuss Gassbag Richard the Se-cunt."	"Shall we play the wantons with our woes, and make some pretty match with shedding tears?"
Wally (Leave it to Beaver)	Chronically overestimates countermeasures that father will take when he hears about this.	"Geez, Beav, Dad's gonna *kill* you."

---

cents!! That's how much.

Cast photos like the one I wanted to include are all over the internet, in many cases used without permission and probably without consequence. But I am too fine a person, and too big a wussie to engage in that sort of petty criminality. But you know what I'm not too big a wussie to do? I'm not too big a wussie to say, Suck it Getty Images! Yes, you heard me! I said *Suck it, Getty Images!* I said it right here in the small print of a footnote in the middle of a book that no one will buy.

Bonus Points	Mitigating Factor
Character gets resurrected at Queen Elizabeth's insistence for further humiliation in shitty sequel *The Merry Wives of Windsor*, is routinely mocked by underlings.	Actually *has* underlings; is relatively kind to sex workers; dies in bed surrounded by loved ones.
Survives to end of epic tetralogy in the course of which anyone with a trace of dignity has been butchered.	Inappropriate and incomprehensible outbursts suggest undiagnosed Tourette's Syndrome.
There are two of them.	Not too proud to share a kitchen maid.
Assassination turns out to have been a zany mix-up!	At least got Shakespeare play named after self—more than that rugged show-off Richard the Lionheart can say.
Is putty in the hands of Mary Ellen Rogers.	Counterintuitive friendship with E. Haskell bodes well for future.

Character (Work)	Wuss Credentials	Signature Line
Antigonus (*The Winter's Tale*)	Abandons an innocent infant just because his boss tells him to; can't make his wife shut up; is so loathed by his own creator that Shakespeare has him torn apart by a wild animal.	*"Ahhhhhhhhh!"*
Sir Andrew Aguecheek (*Twelfth Night*)	Where to begin? Blinks first in swordfight with a girl; is taken for all his money by supposed friends; emptily threatens lawsuits.	"I was adored once, too."
Malcolm (*Macbeth*)	Flees country after father's murder, leaving it at the mercy of a Clintonesque demonically possessed power couple; leads assault on enemy castle while hiding behind a portable forest.	"I am as yet unknown to woman."
Hamlet (*Hamlet*)	Inadvertently wipes out entire family of annoying but innocent bystanders during long, self-absorbed reverie.	"Oh what a rogue and peasant slave am I."
Larry Mondello (*Leave it to Beaver*)	Flees home when caught reading sister's diary; is deemed unworthy by Beaver of membership in the Bloody Five.	"Beaver punched me in the stomach, right where I almost had my operation!"

Bonus Points	Mitigating Factor
You know you're a loathsomely spineless character when Shakespeare washes his hands of you with the hastily scribbled stage direction *Exit, chased by a bear.* "So, you want us to dress some guy up in a bear suit, eh?" you can hear the incredulous wardrobe master asking. No, Shakespeare replied, "I want a fresh actor eaten alive just off-stage by a bear every night." The man knew how to pack a theater.	Hey, you wouldn't be able to make his wife shut up either.
Genuinely likes to dance.	Has engaged in bear-baiting and lived to tell of it: Take *that*, Antigonus.
In a play littered with corpses, fails to kill anybody at all.	Assumes throne at end, but won't last long if witches have anything to say about it.
Harbors creepy fixation on mother's sex life—and tells her so!	Chats up a ghost while his bodyguards tremble.
Appears in a couple dozen episodes but never slays anyone, not even the eminently slayable Whitey Whitney.	Conspires Cassius-like with Eddie against Wally; cuts rather a manly figure when standing beside Whitey.

Character (Work)	Wuss Credentials	Signature Line
Puck *(Midsummer Night's Dream)*	Absorbs mentor's abuse, then takes frustration out on helpless lower species.	"We'll try no manhood here."
Caliban (aka "The Monster") *(The Tempest)*	In Monster hierarchy, only slightly more terrifying than Telly; signature gesture is a shivering cringe.	"Do not torment me, prithee; I'll bring my wood home faster."
Ward *(Leave it to Beaver)*	Punishments never measure up to apocalyptic expectations; allows son to be called "Beaver."	"Oh, *Beaver!* Your mother and I have been very patient with you…"
Casca *(Julius Caesar)*	Fails so miserably in role of lead-off stabber that Caesar is still spouting famous lines six gashes later.	"It is the part of men to fear and tremble, when the most mighty gods by tokens send such dreadful heralds to astonish us."

Bonus Points	Mitigating Factor
Actually apologizes to audience for offending.	Outranks fairies and lets them know it.
Regards drunken sailor as his god.	Dreadful personal hygiene doesn't stop him from putting moves on hot human teen.
Unable to come to grips with physical needs of hellcat wife.	Could still kick shit out of Mr. Brady or the dad on *The O.C.* if it came to that.
Aforesaid fearing and trembling is all on account of a thunderstorm.	To his credit, this particular thunderstorm features people strolling about with their bodies aflame and the odd lion thrown in.

8. *Profiles in Wussitude, Vol. 2*

The Imperial Wuss

Born and painstakingly bred to be the living embodiment of godlike manliness in a warrior society, Hirohito poses to some historians the question "Can a man be at once an unindicted war criminal responsible for the slaughter of millions *and* a colossal wussie?"

That question will not be answered here nor even seriously considered, because as astute readers will have by now noticed, it's not that kind of book. We will, however, consider the life of

Hirohito, aka the Emperor Showa of Japan (1901-1989), as an object lesson to all wussies that one can live long and prosper even as events transpiring all around one go horribly, horribly wrong.

Part 1. Barely Bearable Forebears

In 1901 Hirohito was, to his subsequent lifelong regret, born. As if to add insult to injury, he found himself born into an ancient line of imperial rulers of Japan, much as Isaac before him had unwittingly been born into the biblical patriarch business.

But while Isaac had had to contend from infancy with the constant threat posed by a knife-wielding lunatic of a father, Hirohito was kept at a safe distance from his whip-wielding lunatic of a father by cooler heads. Humanity had come a long way in the intervening seven or eight millennia, ensuring that Hirohito had things just a tad easier. Moreover, Isaac was saddled with a father who was no mere madman but also a towering historical figure whose shadow could never be outrun. Hirohito's father, in contrast, was a mere madman.

Indeed, the historical legacy of Yoshihito, aka the Emperor Taisho, begins and ends with nostril-flaring, eye-bugging, booger-baking, jibber-jabbering, naked-jumping-jacking, rolling-in-horse-manure battiness. Let us consider his story first.

—¤—

The product of a coupling of Emperor Meiji and one of his spiffier concubines, young Yoshihito did not last long in a classroom environment and had to be privately tutored. One suspects that the incessant *yo'-mama's-a-concubine* gibes played no small role in this estrangement from his peers and subsequent mental health issues. He grew up to believe that he was Kaiser Wilhelm of Germany and that everyone he met was Kaiser Wilhelm's horse. His reviews of the troops tended to devolve into spontaneous pieces of performance art wherein he would stop to whip a random soldier, then make amends farther down the line by stopping again to pet and cuddle another one.

It was agreed by all concerned best to keep him out of sight after his first official act as emperor, the opening of the 1913 Diet, ended prematurely with him rolling his prepared speech into a telescope through which he peered suspiciously at his audience. The most noteworthy event of his fourteen-year reign was the devastating earthquake that flattened Tokyo in 1923. That was not Emperor Taisho's fault, but it did nothing for his image. Eventually the court elders shunted him away to a home near the beach stocked with more concubines than he could shake a whip at.

For Taisho's son Hirohito, in what would prove to be the first big piece of rotten luck in a lifelong run of it, the seeming good fortune of having a pygmy of a father to follow would ultimately backfire. For so unspeakably awful had been the reign of Emperor Taisho that the aristocracy and public alike preferred to pretend that it had simply never happened. For Japan, the Taisho Period was the equivalent of *Rocky V* for Sylvester Stallone fans or the 2008 NFL season for Detroit Lions supporters. And once it was agreed upon that there really had been no Taisho Period, that it was all just a bad dream, young Hirohito found himself the object of comparisons with his grandfather, the Emperor Meiji. And that was very bad news for him.

—◻—

To the general public, Meiji was the revered mover and shaker of the Meiji Restoration and its attendant abolition of feudalism, the martial mastermind behind the nation's triumphs in its wars with China and Russia, the promulgator of its first constitution, and the all-around good guy and Renaissance Man who had dragged the nation kicking and screaming out of medieval darkness and into the bright sunshine of industrialization and worldwide respect. Those who knew him personally revered him for his avid consumption of fine whiskeys and concubines, and for the vast quantities of lively semen that he deposited in them.*

The Emperor Meiji went through favorite concubines the way George Steinbrenner would go through Yankee managers a century later. There was Lady Mitsuko, who lasted barely a season before dying in childbirth (the equivalent of missing the playoffs); then came Lady Natsuko, who left after two years and a single stillborn child. Lady Naruko had a heady six-year run highlighted by the birth of a future emperor and two siblings, but was prone to torrid, drunken tirades against the Boss that led to her ouster.†

The more composed Lady Kotoko was then brought in for three seasons until it became clear that she was only good for churning out daughters. Finally there came Lady Sachiko, the Joe Torre of this analogy, who toughed it out for fourteen years and eight offspring until Meiji hung up the penile suction pump and retired from reproductive fornication at forty-four in order to devote his final fifteen years to full-time drinking.‡

Part 2. Mentors and Mushrooms

So this was the image that the young Hirohito had to measure up to, winning-the-public's-respect-and-affection-wise. He would find himself, as others had already found him, not particularly well equipped for that task. The adjectives one finds applied to the young Hirohito in biographies include "reticent," "docile,"

---

* The concubines, that is, and not, so far as we know, the whiskeys.

† No, wait—that was Billy Martin. The two are often confused.

‡ Watching from the sidelines throughout the decades in a sort of general manager's role was the emperor's wife Haruko, who produced no children at all. Relieved from the twin burdens of sex and childbearing by Japan's refreshingly liberal rules of royal succession, she was free to pursue any hobbies she might have had, be they tea ceremony, flower arrangement, or plotting the deaths of concubines.

"physically weak," "nervous," "clumsy," "anxious," "hesitant," "maladroit," "impressionable," and "puny." The traits he was considered to lack included "martial spirit," "calmness," "a proper imperial demeanor," and "intellectual curiosity."[*]

When he was about twelve months old, other toddlers were brought in to play with him. Though of the same age, these infants were generally much bigger than the future emperor and had a tendency to take away his toys, after which the offending youngsters were taken aside and quietly executed.[†]

Later in childhood, one of his instructors, a Mr. Naito, led him on a midwinter nature walk, in the midst of which Hirohito was forced to stand stock-still under an icy waterfall for fifteen minutes as a character-building exercise. At the end of the quarter hour, the future emperor bowed to the instructor and accepted a towel. Yes, that's right: one of his earliest nemeses was a species of PE teacher; and I don't know what more the reader could hope for in terms of bona fide wussie street-cred.

The lad found a father figure in the great Russo-Japanese war hero Admiral Nogi, one of many esteemed gentlemen entrusted with his training and development, who met with Hirohito almost daily from the time he was seven. For years Nogi proved to be a kind and upright guiding force for the boy, his only character flaw being a nasty habit of murdering his wife and committing ritual suicide every time an emperor died, which inevitably happened with the keeling over of Hirohito's grandfather Meiji.

Hirohito's wacky father, supposing the lad to be devastated by the losses of both his grandfather and beloved tutor, sought to console him by dispatching to him one of his favorite concubines. Hirohito, eleven at the time, presumably showed her his butterfly collection, for natural history had by this time become his passion.

The successor to Nogi as favorite (or at least least-loathed) mentor was Dr. Hattori, his natural history tutor, who would lead

---

[*] Bonus points on "calmness": that one came from his mom.

[†] Not really.

him to the hills for pleasant days collecting specimens. In addition to butterflies, fungi became an object of fascination for the new crown prince. There was, however, one particular phylum of clingy parasite that he could not abide, namely the court officials who would shadow him everywhere, even on these nature outings.

By his early teens, Hirohito wasn't exactly a big fan of humans, and can you blame him? If humans weren't stealing his toys, they were ordering him under waterfalls. If they weren't indulging themselves in murder-suicide pacts, they were dumping their leftover concubines on him. The mushrooms never pulled any of that crap on you. He vented his frustration re humans to Hattori, whom he regarded as an exception that proves the rule.

"I hear you, little dude," Hattori said. (I'm paraphrasing.) "And you know what? I know this great place for getting away from humans. It's big and it's not too hard to get to. It's called the ocean!"

Thus began weekly excursions to the seaside town of Hayama, where a boat would take mentor and pupil out for hours of skin-diving for pearls and other specimens. To his delight, teenaged Hirohito found the undersea world to be indeed a human-free zone, its only drawback being the limited time he could spend there before necessity forced him back to the cruel, cold, human-infested surface.

Despite all the efforts made by his childhood tutors to build up his constitution, the only impressive physical feat that he would ever demonstrate was an ability to hold his breath for very long periods.

Part 3. Jerky Boy

Eventually he would have to emerge from the depths, of course, and when he did, the humans would be waiting, now more eager than ever to buck him up and hasten his maturation as he lurched spasmodically toward adulthood. And always with the same imperfect results.

It was often a case of too many cooks. A certain General Nara, another veteran of the Russo-Japanese War brought in as nineteen-year-old Hirohito's military coach, had a trench dug inside the prince's compound so that the young man could practice firing machine guns. The general was dismayed when a bleeding-heart faction of court officials vetoed a plan to allow Hirohito to mow down live game on the theory that it "would harm the moral sensibilities of an emperor."

Despite such schisms, a consensus soon coalesced around the idea that a trip abroad would help stabilize Hirohito's wobbly character. The education he was getting at home clearly wasn't cutting it. Nara complained about the prince's random, jerky body movements and his shrill, non-imperial voice. This observation aroused the jealousy of other advisors, in whose presence Hirohito never spoke at all, even when asked direct questions. So everyone agreed that a change of scenery might be just the thing to jolt him out of his shell.

The United States as a destination was ruled out from the get-go: the ambassador to Washington cabled his superiors in Tokyo that the prince would not be able to cope with "the rough behavior of ordinary Americans," particularly newspaper reporters. And so at twenty, the heir to the throne was packed off to Europe for six months—first and foremost to England, where print journalists have always been renowned for their kid-glove treatment of royalty.

Nonetheless, nothing was left to chance. Two expert handlers would accompany the crown prince every step of the way on his five-nation tour, and these handlers had handlers of their own. One of the handler handlers—indeed, the uber-handler handler—was Prime Minister Hara, who instructed the hands-on handlers as follows:

Regarding the crown prince's habits, such as his frequent body movements, I want everyone in attendance close to him to correct this.

—□—

The British admire the Stiff Upper Lip—at least, that was the operative stereotype during this prewar era. Metaphorically speaking, Hirohito had the stiffest of upper lips. But physically? Not so much. That carp about frequent body moments wasn't as callous as it may seem, especially where the upper lip was concerned. Throughout Hirohito's life that upper lip trembled. It flapped. It twitched—a lot. It roiled and ruffled and rattled. It rose and fell, wiggled and waggled, twisted and shouted. At some point in its highly aerobic career it must have attained every attribute possible for an upper lip with the glaring exception of stiffness.

As soon as he was able, Hirohito cultivated a mustache. We can only speculate as to why he did so. Given that handlers meddled in every aspect of his life from his daily wardrobe to his choice of bride, we have to wonder whether the mustache was entirely his own idea. We can speculate that the mustache was a stratagem on his part—or on someone's part—to cover the renegade lip, perhaps in hopes of tamping it down, anchoring it. If so, that scheme backfired as badly as the later attack on Pearl Harbor, since the centipede-like addition to the young emperor's face only served to call more attention to the turbulent flap of flesh that lurked beneath it. The bushier the thing became with age, the worse the distraction.

Unstiff upper lip notwithstanding, the Brits took to the youngster as soon as he arrived, and he to them. Years later he would cite this 1921 visit to England as the giddiest time of his life.

On his first morning in Buckingham Palace, King George V, only half-dressed in carpet slippers and an open shirt, barged into Hirohito's suite before breakfast and horrified the imperial handlers by slapping the prince on the back and declaring, "I hope, my boy, that everyone is giving you everything that you want while you are here. If there is anything you need, just ask. I'll never forget how your grandfather treated me and my brother when we were in Yokohama!" All of which Hirohito heard as:

Drizzle Drazzle Drozzle Drome. Prufrock plucks at Cotton Mather wringing his anatomy on the Westinghouse. Yippi-yi-ki-yay, Mather plucker. Yabba-dabba-doo to you too, Dino.

Much of what we know about Hirohito's European adventure comes to us filtered through the diary compiled by his two clingiest handlers, and thus retains the unique flavor and aroma of an expertly concocted and ever-so-delicately seasoned bullshit soufflé. Here's a typical serving:

His Highness has shown great skill in conducting conversations with the great statesmen of England. The way in which he talked with Mr. Lloyd George was something which could hardly be emulated by professional diplomats… In parting His Highness said: "I am told you are frightfully busy these days. I hope you will take very good care of yourself not only for the good of this country, but also in the interests of the rest of the world." The British Prime Minister was deeply moved by these words of His Highness.

Hirohito's principal native companion during his time in England, the Prince of Wales, was fated never to encounter this eloquent Oriental whiz kid who could wring tears from flinty prime ministers. The Hirohito who tagged along with him to restaurants and nightclubs and golf courses and hunting fields barely spoke, and Prince Edward seems to have regarded his companion as something akin to that dorky, forgettable second cousin who shows up in your dorm one hungover Sunday morning with a note from your mom pinned to his chest commanding you to take him around the campus and show him a good time—if, that is, the dorky second cousin came equipped with a band of jittery handlers constantly hovering over him.

Edward did warm to his guest on one occasion: A newspaper published a cheeky report asserting that the visitor from Japan could not possibly be true royalty and must be an impostor sent by the Japanese government as a provocative diplomatic insult. On a train from Windsor to London, Edward remarked, "I hear you aren't really here. It's the first time I've ever been out with a ghost. May I touch you? Ha! Ha! Ha!" all of which Hirohito heard as:

Buy me a eunuch, ee-ii, ee-ii. Oh. And on this dime he shat a roast. Knick! Knack paddy-whack! Deviate woof! Brains taper thwart? Arf! Arf! Arf!

But the language barrier could not keep Hirohito from marveling at the relative freedom enjoyed by his counterpart. The entourage-free Edward could drop into some random dive for a spot of champagne, could ask pretty girls to dance with him, could swear out loud. He could ride a horse or swim or do anything else listed in the promotional copy on a box of quality tampons. Hirohito never got over this awakening-from-the-Matrix experience, though one is left yearning to know just what sort of utterance he might have made if given full license to swear. The aftermath of the Battle of Midway would have been as good a time as any to sound him on that.

Part 4. Party Like It's 1929

Energized by his European escapades, Hirohito returned home determined to redefine the position of crown prince of Japan. On a wildhair, he decided to throw a party and not tell his parents! With drinks! And music! And chicks! Just the sort of thing you or I might have done in our high school days, except that he was twenty when he finally got around to it.

He got the idea from his role model, the Prince of Wales, who was always rounding up a bunch of fun-loving kids and throwing records on the phonograph and doing the Charleston with short-skirted debutantes who called him Edward, just Edward. Not that Hirohito ever witnessed any of these shindigs firsthand—for whatever reason (simple oversight, one supposes) he had not been invited—but surely his good friend Edward wouldn't exaggerate.

So he asked a bunch of his classmates from college over and

insisted that they stop groveling to him, and when they wouldn't or couldn't stop, when they kept bowing and muttering "Yes, Your Highness, we shall endeavor to cease groveling to Your Highness, begging Your Highness's pardon," he called in the heavy artillery in the form of a keg of real Scotch, brewed by a real Scotsman originally for another Scotsman, but given to him instead in order to commemorate his visit to Scotland.

And that worked well enough, but there was still one problem, namely: just who was it that these lubricated ex-grovelers were expected to dance with? Hirohito didn't know any chicks. He had a fiancée by this time, but was barely on speaking terms with her. Some of those concubines that were always being chucked in his path would have come in handy now, but instead he called in a few geisha,* and oh Lordy if a back-slappin', whiskey-swillin', geisha-oglin', toilet-pukin' good time was not had by all—until Dad found out.

Actually, Dad didn't find out, he was too busy secreting walnuts in his underpants down at the beach house, but Prince Saionji, Hirohito's head caretaker, did, and boy was he pissed! Not by the drinking nor by the geishas, mind you, but by the whole concept of Hirohito's trying to get people to stop groveling to him after it had been so darned hard to get them to start.

So a chastened Hirohito gave up on the idea of partying like the Prince of Wales and instead had himself a nine-hole golf course built on the palace grounds so that he could dress up like the Prince of Wales and play it. Alone.

And he kept on playing saucy tunes on the gramophone like the Prince of Wales did. But in private.

And he insisted on being served bacon and eggs for breakfast whenever possible for the rest of his life, like the Prince of Wales was. To eat by himself.

Ha. That would show them…

---

* …who, despite their reputation in the West, are in fact not nearly as flexible or fun as concubines

Part 5. Color Blind Love

At this point a picture of the young prince's life begins to emerge that is just too sad and lonely to contemplate. But no need to worry; as tends to be the case with crown princes as a class, there were people charged with making sure that he would not lack for companionship. A lot of such people, in fact—mainly the parents of girls of a suitable age to become his princess.

The fact that he became engaged to a fifteen-year-old becomes significantly less creepy when one learns that he himself was seventeen at the time. Then again, it ratchets quickly back up to full-on creepy again when one delves into the selection process: His mother corralled all the likely candidates into the palace for a tea party and arranged for Hirohito to peep on them from a secret vantage point.

This whole escapade enraged one faction of the aristocracy, not because it was creepy and secretive but because it was insufficiently so. Hirohito's father and grandfather had not been allowed to peep on their fiancées prior to their betrothals, so what made this young buck think he was so special, demanded this faction. On top of which, the enraged faction had a princess candidate of its own who had been shut out.

In a further jaw-dropping break with tradition, the young lady chosen by the prince—Nagako by name—was actually *informed* of her fate and brought in to meet her future husband before any announcements were made. This initial encounter went well, at least by the standards of Hirohito's encounters with humans, as evidenced by the fact that he willingly met with Nagako a second time three weeks later for the taking of engagement photos, and then as many as nine more times over the next seven years of their betrothal, which seemed about right to him, quality-time-with-fiancée-wise.

The engagement might have been a bit more concise but for the unseemly maneuverings of the aforementioned enraged faction—the one whose own princess candidate had been checked into the boards, as it were. They arranged to have a nasty article published in a medical journal during the third year of the engagement which revealed that on Nagako's mother's side there ran an insidious streak of—brace yourself for it—*color-blindness*. This, of course, rendered her entirely unsuitable for marriage to the twitchy, uncommunicative son of a nutty alcoholic horn-dog.

Months of bitter, accusatory letter writing between the factions ensued, followed by death threats, suicide threats, and the machinations of something called the Black Dragon Society. All the while, no one bothered to ask Hirohito or Nagako what they might have wanted to do. Nagako and her family, as well as the rival faction, waited for the quiet young man to tip his hand. What was he thinking? Which family would he ultimately side with? What intrigues were boiling beneath the silent surface of the crown prince?

It turns out that when the going gets tough, the not-at-all-tough go skin diving. Then they flee to Europe.

But for what it's worth, throughout the ordeal, Hirohito kept telling anyone who would listen to him that he still wanted *that* female human, Nagako, and not any of the ringers constantly being dangled before him. Presumably he continued to feel this way during his tour of Europe, but declined to let his fiancée in on the secret via so much as a postcard. He did, however, bring back a bitchin' set of bagpipes for his future father-in-law.

Finally, all the celestial signs were aligned for a happy wedding in 1923, and then that danged killer earthquake hit, postponing everything for yet another year. The two crazy kids finally tied the knot in January 1924 at the ripe old ages of twenty-two and twenty.

Part 6. Oh My Darlin' Concubine

A mere two years of feverish, court-ordered intercourse later, Hirohito's seed found purchase. The nation waited with the proverbial bated breath for the birth of another future emperor, but upon her arrival in December 1926 she lacked the penis which for thousands of years had usually been considered a prerequisite for the position. A British journalist noted that ordinary subjects greeted one another on the street with arms raised, shouting *Banzai!* in the traditional mode of greeting the news of an imperial birth. But as everyone was well aware of the gender of the child, "these were tepid banzais."*

Let us pause here to review how succession worked in those days. As we have already learned, Hirohito's grandfather Meiji's visits to his legal spouse's vagina could best be described as cameo appearances. But as honorary coach of the palace concubine squad, Meiji had given his all to raising morale and giving everyone playing time. For all the emperoring duties he was obliged to fulfill as the Architect of Modern Japan, he was never too busy to show a shy newcomer the ropes.

Meiji's son Taisho (aka Yoshihito) had actually gone through his wife to bring forth Hirohito, but this was something of a happy accident given the father's diminished capacity for distinguishing women from fillies. Throughout the late Emperor Taisho's reign, court concubines might have worried about any number of things—indiscriminate whippings, being force-fed raw carrots— but job security was not among their concerns.

Therefore, it was not entirely surprising under the circumstances that with this first failure out of the box (if you'll pardon the expression), the pressure would mount on Nagako to produce a proper penis-bearing heir, lest she be benched in favor of new talent.

For his part, Hirohito, emulating the nurse shark, stuck rigorously to a biennial mating pattern, producing children again in 1927, 1929, and 1931—all, alas, girls. With every daughter, court officials clucked their tongues ever louder at Nagako's incompetent processing of perfectly good imperial sperm while the public's

---

* I know—you are not alone. I, too, spent five minutes after I read that account pacing my living room and trying to pull off a tepid banzai. It's a fruitless enterprise, though oddly addictive.

*banzai*s grew tepid to the point of surliness. *Yeah, yeah, yeah. Banzai to you, too, dickwad.* Through it all, Hirohito stood by his wife. This failed to impress snippy court officials quick to point out that he might more efficiently impregnate Nagako if he stopped standing by her and got busy lying on her.

But Nagako already had enough weight pressing down on her without the addition of a spindly emperor, for ultimately she bore the brunt of the blame for all these superfluous princesses littering the palace. Although Hirohito had, upon ascending the throne, abolished the imperial concubinage, there were still plenty of free agents roaming about, each with her own high-powered rep. If Nagako failed to deliver the goods one more time, these nubile hordes were sure to be unleashed on Hirohito whether he liked it or not. Everything depended on the next child, scheduled for delivery in (you guessed it) 1933.

—◻—

It should be obvious at this point in the narrative that I, as a wussie, identify powerfully with Hirohito. His story up to this age is—in a surprising number of ways—my story and perhaps your story, too. And yet I must confess to finding it hard to empathize with our hero on this whole concubine issue. I'm afraid he and I part company here.

I don't doubt that Nagako had her good points. For one thing, there was documented proof that she could distinguish all major colors. And photographs taken in her prime reveal a girl who emits a certain unique and mushroom-like allure. One can certainly see where she might have sparked a raging imperial boner every couple of years or so.

Even so, had I found myself in Hirohito's position in the fall of 1933, I for one have to admit to you that I would have been pulling for one more daughter. My interior cheerleader would have been all, like, *Gimme an X! Gimme another X!*

Not Hirohito. He was made of sterner stuff, upper lip notwithstanding, and Nagako rewarded his touching loyalty by bringing forth that year the future emperor Akihito.

And she wasn't done yet. In a blatant in-your-face to those lurking wannabe concubines, she churned out a backup heir at the end of the next mating cycle in 1935. And after that, one last daughter just for the hell of it.

—◻—

By the time Nagako had gotten the monkey off her back and the twitchy spouse off her front, Emperor Taisho had long since departed for that big stud farm in the sky and Hirohito's reign, aka the Showa Era, was in full swing.*

Alas, Hirohito himself probably shared little of his wife's relief, since his day job was going pretty badly by that time. For one thing, his prime ministers had developed an annoying habit of getting shot. Events were multiplying far beyond the control of your average mild-mannered amateur marine biologist. Herbert P. Bix writes, "It is fair to say that through 1931 Hirohito had less ruled than presided over his people, and that his performance had been dilatory, inconsistent, and self-contradictory." The army, on its own initiative, rolled into Manchuria that summer. A *New York Times* correspondent called Japan a nation of "government by assassination." Sheesh!

After a 1933 imperial audience, US ambassador Joseph C. Grew, demonstrating the very sort of bluntness that had gotten his country blacklisted from the teenaged Hirohito's foreign itinerary, noted that "The Emperor seemed very nervous and twitched more than usual." And of course, as we all know, things started barreling downhill at a faster and faster clip from there onward.

---

* Let me become the one thousand seven hundred and forty-second commentator to note the irony of the selection of the name "Showa," which means "enlightened peace," for Hirohito's tumultuous reign.

Part 7. The War Years: Never Mind

This brings us to the years during which Japan fought a war in China, then entered World War II, and finally saw its empire go up in flames. The degree of responsibility that Hirohito bore for those wars, for atrocities committed during them, and for the havoc wreaked on his own country has been the subject of much speculation, mostly by historians living outside Japan. I would like to point out that I reside *in* Japan, where public figures who have speculated about Hirohito's role in these events have been threatened, shot, or stabbed by fanatics. Thus, you will forgive me for glossing over the subject. I wouldn't be much of a wussie if I didn't, now, would I.

Here's one thing that historians generally agree on: When Hirohito endorsed Japan's surrender, he did so with no inkling as to how the victors would treat him. While hanging couldn't be ruled out, he might well have assumed that his likeliest fate was forced abdication and life in prison. In this hypothetical world, Hirohito would have lived out his days in a small cell with only occasional visits from family and no other human contact whatsoever.

This, to him, would probably not have seemed at all a bad deal. He may have dared to dream that, like his father, he would be banished to a remote seaside cottage where he could pursue his scholarly interest in jellyfish, free from meddling humankind.

Alas, the wily Douglas MacArthur was too clever for him by half. The Supreme Commander not only arranged for Hirohito to remain unindicted but also made sure that none of those who did go to trial got a chance to say anything mean about him. Hirohito could not abdicate, nor would he be allowed to live out his days in splendid seclusion.

Instead, he would be compelled to renounce the divinity that had been ascribed to emperors through the centuries and declare himself a mere human. Surely he must have felt a sharp twinge at this news, not so much for the divinity-renouncing part as for the latter half, for Hirohito would much rather have declared himself a fungus or a jellyfish than a human.

Then came the real blow: His new role in the postwar scheme of things was to serve as a living symbol of the Japanese people—a job that consisted almost in its entirety of...*meeting and talking to other humans.*

Lots and lots and lots of other humans.

Part 8. Embracing Humanity, One Human at a Time

The humans with whom Hirohito was forced to interact fell into two broad categories: ordinary Japanese citizens and visiting foreign dignitaries. It is hard to say which type of encounter was the more painful for him, but judging from the responses of those who partook of Hirohito's society, the dealings with dignitaries were the more colossal failures.

Hirohito took to his ceremonial duties like a duck to quicksand. In later years, the king of Thailand, for one, was rumored to dread the periodic visits to his fellow Asian monarch, not owing to the war nor any perceived personal slight but simply because the host and his whole brood were just so bloody dull.

To his subjects, in contrast, many of whom led fairly dull lives themselves, a little touch of Hiro was usually a welcome if bewildering distraction. Most of them had little difficulty accepting the emperor's new non-divine status. That point had been driven home by the famous photo taken at the Supreme Commander's headquarters in which the overdressed emperor resembles nothing so much as a ventriloquist's dummy that a bored MacArthur has ceased to find amusing. Now, Hirohito's new American handlers with their zany democratic ideals had decided that a series of appearances at ordinary workplaces and public forums was the best way to introduce him to his own nation.

To survive these forced marches through factories, construction sites, art galleries and so forth, he devised a three-part conversational stratagem: His opening gambit was a memorized snippet he had picked up somewhere, along the lines of "What exactly is it that you do here?"; then he would stand back and think about jellyfish until the hands and lips of his interlocutor ceased their curious movements; finally, he would say, *Ah, so desu ka* ("Oh, is that right?"). His subjects, reveling in their newly established right to not only gaze upon their dread liege but to make fun of him as well, semi-affectionately assigned him the nickname "King Is-That-Right?"

Doubtless there was many a moment during an all-morning wood-pulp factory inspection or the third course of a state dinner for an eye-rolling brother monarch when Hirohito cursed that lucky bastard Tojo, who had found blissful oblivion at the end of a hangman's rope back in '48. Meanwhile, the indignities that would be heaped upon him were only beginning.

—◻—

As time passed, Hirohito would make a peace of sorts with his meet-and-greet duties. An apocryphal story is told about a formal welcome ceremony he was to have hosted for a potentate in the Sixties. A couple of chamberlains cornered the emperor in one of his laboratories, wrestled him into a swallow-tail coat and tie, and nudged him toward one of the imperial palace's receiving rooms.

The great double doors were thrown open to reveal a dimly lit chamber devoid of potentates. Devoid of any living soul, for that matter. Hirohito mechanically strode the prescribed number of steps into the vacant room, bowed deeply to the stale air, and then backed silently out. As the chamberlains sheepishly closed the doors behind him, he remarked (so the story goes), "We've got to hold more receptions like this."

I arrived in Japan in 1979, and the Hirohito that I remember was semiannually prodded out onto the balcony of the imperial palace on New Year's Day and on his birthday in April, along with the Empress and their progeny, to be adored by the little-plastic-flag-waving public gathered in the grounds below.

He forever gave the impression of disbelief that the time for this ceremony, which it seemed to him had been dutifully performed only yesterday, had come around again. He would wave stiffly, mustachioed upper lip twitching feverishly away, right hand mechanically moving straight ahead and back again, straight ahead and back again, as if he believed he could knock off as soon as he had completed the number of waves negotiated by his union.

Occasionally he would pivot sideways and, to the TV viewer, appear to be waving frantically at some random member of his own family inches away, who would unflappably continue to smile toward the cameras and wave her hand in that decadent—one might say "European"—side-to-side style of waving that seemed to be all the rage among the postwar set, while Hirohito kept flapping his palm at her as if trying to enliven a dying ember embedded in her collar.

Part 9. …And the Indignities Just Keep on Comin'!

Then in 1988, it was reported that the emperor was ill. It soon became clear that this was not another of his short, cautionary hospitalizations. The nation began to receive daily updates of his temperature, blood pressure, and, ominously, amount of discharged blood. Over time this report became as routine a part of the ten o'clock news as the weather forecast: *Today's high in Tokyo was twenty-five degrees Celsius. In the Emperor, it was thirty-eight-point-two. A warm front is expected to drop two centimeters of rain tomorrow, while His Majesty's anus is expected to drop five more cc's of blood.* No one batted an eye after a while.

I was teaching at D University at the time, and in the autumn, as the emperor's mysterious ailment dragged on, I assigned my all male English Communication class a presentation on "A Person Whom I Admire." I gave them my standard demo presentation on Mark Twain and provided ample preparation time. When I collected topics, I found amid the usual assortment of sports icons and rock stars the name "Emperor Showa." In this competition to be named a hero by his own young subjects, Hirohito was vanquished two votes to one by the Swedish shred guitarist Yngwie Malmsteen—not quite the final indignity that he was to suffer, but a milestone nonetheless.

DU had had a turbulent political history. In the Sixties, leftists had flocked there and some had formed a radical cabal called the "Core Faction," whose members went on to carry out small-scale attacks on various corporate and political targets, including a few limp rocket launches onto the grounds of the Imperial Palace. By the Seventies, such provocations had inevitably inspired a rightist backlash on campus, though this generally took such benign forms as joining the Pep Club and wearing something resembling an American high school marching band uniform to school every day.

The lad who chose to honor Hirohito in his presentation did not wear a band uniform, and anyway, the whole Leftist-Rightist dustup had largely shot its wad by the mid-Eighties, both sides ceding ground to the Don't-Give-a-Crap-About-Anything-ism that tends to accompany prosperity. Still, the boy had a lean and hungry look about him that gave me pause.

On the day of his presentation, this heretofore quiet fellow took to the podium and spoke unwaveringly, in a confident baritone that Hirohito's early handlers might once have yearned to appropriate for him:

"I will give my presentation about the current Japanese emperor."

[Nervous chuckling.]

"The emperor, whose given name is Hirohito, was born in Tokyo in 1901…"

[Chuckling fades.]

Following the formula that I had laid out, the student then led us through the major events of his chosen subject's life. This he did in brisk fashion, using up less than half the required time. He still had over three minutes to fill, with nothing to do but explain his reason for admiring the subject. He segued into a darker mood:

"As you know, the emperor is very sick. Very, very sick."

[Heads are bowed.]

"And thanks to his sickness, we can learn new vocabulary which we had never known before, in both Japanese and English."

[He reaches for some poster boards .]

"For example, *toketsu*: to vomit blood."

[Nervous chuckling returns]

"And *geketsu*: to pass blood."

[He's got them in the palm of his hand now, and continues in his fiery-eyed yet deadpan delivery.]

"The reason I admire the emperor is his great ability to expel blood. I have calculated that during his recent illness, he has expelled more than three times the amount of blood that a man of his size normally carries in his body. Isn't that amazing?"

The audience quickly got into the spirit of the thing in an unusually lively Q-and-A:

"Do you believe the rumor that the emperor has already died and they aren't telling us?"

Not only that, he answered, but they have him cryogenically frozen, in case they need to trot him out for the crowds on New Year's Day.

"In that case, what were the emperor's last words?"

"Ouch... Ouch."

And so we laughed and laughed, two dozen bright young subjects and their teacher, too, who laughed mostly out of relief. We merrily chortled away at the notion that our sovereign liege had been converted to a literal Emperor of Ice Cream. Even this, though, would not be the final indignity.

Part 10. *Police Academy 4* Was Long Gone

All TV stations were compelled to suspend regular programming for a week after his death. Nothing was to be found on any channel but somber music and old newsreels.

The most frequently replayed bit of video was a blotchy black-and-white clip from 1945. Intercut with shots of a series of outdoor loudspeakers taken from various angles in various cities are scenes of ordinary Japanese subjects staggering through the ruins of their fire- and atom-bombed cities, all presumably taken on the same hot, clear August day at high noon. The pre-recorded voice of Hirohito, screechy and shrill and tremulous, begins to pour forth. It is his famous surrender speech, in which he informs the nation that...

The war situation has developed not necessarily to our advantage.

...causing the subjects, perched upon the rubble that was until recently their homes, their faces twisted in a mixture of shame and awe, to begin weeping at the realization that their monarch has set for all time a standard for understatement that can never be approached. This was also the first time that any of them had heard the voice of an emperor, so there was that, too.

This surrender speech montage makes for powerful television the first time one sees and hears it, but its efficacy tends to wear thin somewhere into the third day of near nonstop rebroadcasting. I visited three video rental stores, all manned by appropriately grim-faced staff, all eerily silent, and all picked clean. What this meant in that grim week of January 1989 was that somewhere in the Nakano Ward of Tokyo, one family of the late emperor's subjects, dumbstruck with bereavement, was watching *National Lampoon's Vacation*, while another was trying to drown its grief through *Spaceballs*.

And that, I sure do hope, was the final indignity.

9. Wussies and Swearing:

Three Moderately Diverting Anecdotes

1. European

A delightful young lady named Bonnie Van Blerkum told me the first dirty joke I remember.

"There's an African in the bedroom," she began, as we skipped together across the blacktopped elementary school playground, Bonnie gesticulating toward rooms in an imaginary house with her dainty right hand. "There's an Asian in the kitchen. Who's in the bathroom?"

I admitted my ignorance.

"European!"

I stared at her, slack-jawed.

"Doncha get it? *Yer-a-peein'!*"

All right, so it's not a very *dirty* dirty joke, but what with the geography lesson embedded in it, a pretty sophisticated one for a first grader. In retrospect, I particularly admire the way she opened with the African in the bedroom—misdirecting me into anticipating the sort of coarse ethnic humor that I had already come to expect from the likes of Darryl Westhuizen—before blindsiding me with the toilet-humor-cum-wordplay roundhouse.

I would spend a considerable amount of time staring slack-jawed at Bonnie Van Blerkum over the next eleven years of our shared K-12 education, always in the hope that one day she would again talk dirty to me. In this desire, as in so many others, I was destined to go almost totally unrequited.

The lone exception came late one night in our junior year of high school at Haag's Cafe. The sunny little jokester from the playground was now a sullen, sardonic teen in an incongruously cheery sky-blue waitress uniform. I watched her from the dishwasher's station as she dragged herself toward one of her booths and flicked a check in the general direction of a burly middle-aged solo diner.

Suddenly he lashed out and seized her wrist. It then appeared that I would at last have the chance to act out my decade-old fantasy of extracting Bonnie from peril and winning the gratitude that she would express in ways that had grown progressively more lurid over the years. But of course I wussied out and peeped around a corner as she effortlessly extricated herself.

"Oh, he just thought I said *Fuck you* to him instead of 'Thank you,'" she explained later.

"And did you?"

"Oh, hell, no," she snorted. "I don't think so, anyway. I made him apologize. Then he gave me a huge tip."

I thought her magnificent.

2. Lady Parts

One sultry Saturday afternoon at Penniman's house in the summer following our high school graduation, some of us were shooting baskets in a desultory manner while others milled around farther down the driveway talking cars, girls, futures.

Among us this day was one Artie Oglesby: a two-time all-state wrestler in the one hundred thirty pound class, a veritable pinning machine and, paradoxically, a wussie. We never understood just what sort of demons possessed Artie when he took to the mat, but they clearly deserted him the moment he triumphantly stepped off. And personally, I was glad of that; the last thing one wants in a friend is an irrepressible impulse to apply headlocks and hip-tosses at random moments, such as in the midst of the game of HORSE we were currently engrossed in.

One look at Artie, though, and any such fears evaporated. Atop his small frame—still sinewy several months after his final match—sat a pale, freckled, pumpkin crowned with shaggy blond hair. He never had an unkind word for anyone, was liked though unsought by female peers, would pet stray cats and turn the other cheek if they scratched the first one. He went to church on Sunday mornings and returned for superfluous Wednesday-night booster shots.

That summer, to his family's chagrin, he took on a cigarette habit while working a factory job. But even in this, his motive was telling: He deliberately selected Old Golds to addict himself to, he said, because no one else on his shift bought them, causing him to "feel sorry" for the shunned brand.[*]

Many of us were doing summer jobs in factories prior to leaving for college. The booming economy of the era encouraged it and so did our parents, the theory being that a dose of exposure to blue-collar lifers and their milieu would inspire us to study hard to avoid their fate. In fact, we were enchanted by the vivid and earthy adults to whom we were being exposed for the first time in our lives.

During a lull in the HORSE action, I told Artie about my recent experience in the factory restroom. I stood at a urinal, trying to ignore the horrific odor emanating from one of the stalls behind me. Asking whether my anonymous colleague was slaughtering a cow in there or what seemed a perfectly reasonable course of action, though I would feel right glad that I refrained when the stall

---

[*] I haven't seen Artie since the dawn of the Internet age, but it would not surprise me a bit to learn that he has taken pity on more than one desperate Nigerian civil servant by now.

door burst open and out came a wiry, pompadoured ex-con, notorious for his temper. He sidled up to me as if reading my thoughts and then informed me:

"IF I DON'T STINK WHEN I SHIT, THEN IT AIN'T WORTH SHITTIN'!"

To which policy I could but nod.

I asked Artie if he, too, had experienced any such meaningful encounters at his gauge- and pump-making facility. He had.

"This guy comes up to me the other day. Like, this old lifer guy? With this scraggly white beard? Drives a forklift?" he began. "I see him around every day, but he never, like, talked to me before. And then, I'm just standin' at my machine? You know, like, settin' it up?" Here his voice drops to a whisper about three notches below the volume of his standard whisper. "And he comes up to me and he goes…he goes:

"'When she's young, it's a *pussy*.

"'When she's middle-aged, it's a *cunt*.

"'And when she's old, it's a *snatch*.'"

Here Artie required a pause to draw two breaths—perhaps those Old Golds were starting to take their toll—before concluding: "And then he just walks away!"

When our host, Penniman, finished consulting on an automotive surgery and joined us, I coaxed Artie into repeating his story. He began eagerly enough, but upon running up against those three keywords again his voice faded, his eyes fluttered, his flesh reddened. It was as if Artie thought that he could slip the words past God if he uttered them softly and contritely enough.

Penniman, a regular churchgoer himself, thoroughly enjoyed the anecdote—enough so to call the others around for another encore performance. By this time, Artie was feeling the power of the words. His tongue lasciviously lingered over each *p* and *s* and *c* and *n* and every low vowel, the way a starving man might roll the first bite of a juicy sirloin around his mouth before starting to chew.

We all agreed that, odd as the encounter was, it was by no means unenlightening. We were suddenly made aware of the fact that each of us had on occasion wondered what we were to do with this plethora of synonyms for the same female body part, and now an elder of our tribe had elected to step forward with practical rules of usage. As these encounters go, Artie's vocabulary lesson carried much more practical value than, say, learning of a co-worker's preference for malodorous bowel movements.

As to why the elder had chosen Artie Oglesby as his prophet, well, that was not for us to know. We had to accept such wisdom with gratitude whenever and wherever we could get it. Perhaps he knew that his message would be retold, and that, for someone like Artie, the chance to say those words—sanctioned somehow by their encasement in quotation marks—afforded him a more palpable and giddy sort of excitement than taking down a cocky big-city opponent at State ever did.

I for one still can't usually bring myself to use any of those words, but have been known to correct others when I hear one of them used improperly. "Now, now. You can't say *snatch* with regard to Paris Hilton," I'll chide. "Not yet, anyway."

3. City of Angels

Since I acquired full-time faculty status, both universities that have employed me have granted me an annual allowance for attending academic conferences related to my field. I consider my yearly conference trips to be not so much career-enhancement opportunities as marriage-preservation ones, and so I shop for a conference in an exotic locale where I can take Mrs. Muggins along with me.

Our favorite destination is the capital of Thailand, which annually hosts a convention of sufficient relevance to my specialty. We love that steamy metro-pot: love the swelter, the restaurants, the kindness toward strangers of its people, but most of all—at least in my case—just love *saying* it.

Every time we embark on a trip to Thailand, or even discuss the plans for it, I can't help going out of my way to mention that city, the formal Thai name of which translates as City of Angels. For example, I'll check the forecast before we depart so as to inform Mrs. Muggins that "good weather awaits us in Bang…*kok*." Or as we walk its streets, I might note, "Wow, the air in Bang…*kok* doesn't seem as bad as it was last time we were here. Here in Bang…*kok*, that is." And later I'll be apt to lament that "Gee, I'll sure be sorry to leave good ol' Bang…*kok*. Won't you?"

Inevitably, there comes the moment when she moans, "Would you *please* stop saying Bang…*kok?*"

But then, she has said it, too.

10. Playing the Wussie Card

I am looking at the Jack of Clubs with unqualified, teeth-baring loathing. Disdain seeps through my being virally, cell by revolted cell, as I scan the dismal geography of his flat form. There is no redeeming value to be found in this most knavish of knaves. I despise him from the tip of his crown down to...well, the tip of his other crown.

Just look at this mope; I mean really. Just *look* at that face. Lay him down amid his ostensible peers and compare. The Jack of Diamonds oozes wealth and savoir faire; he'd have no trouble at all seducing the Queen of any suit—or the King, for that matter. The Jacks of Hearts and Spades, those dashing Wild Card Boys, exchange a shrewd wink with their unseen eyes, for they know full well how *every* game is played and won, and a lack of organs below the waist isn't about to slow these lotharios down, eh? Adapt and overcome, that's their motto.

And then there is our boy Clubby, with his stooped posture and hangdog air of doom. The lowest ranking of the face cards and damn well aware of it, he has long since abandoned all hope of promotion. His King, meanwhile, looks to be contemplating *hara-kiri* with an upraised sword, such is the throbbing intensity of his disappointment with his son and sole heir.

On the Wikipedia page for Jacks—the existence of which perhaps surprises no one in this day and age—there is a photo of someone fanning the knavish foursome into a poker hand. The Jack of Clubs is tucked between his two red cousins in such a way that his face—and only *his* face—is obscured. This is not a coincidence. It can't be.

He makes me want to throw up, the Jack of Clubs does. He is not real, cannot even claim the quasi-real status of a vivid fictional character, and yet I yearn to somehow breathe life into him only for the pleasure of watching him flail on the floor like the worthless, legless, helpless wussie-freak that he is, and then to summarily execute him, putting him out of his whiney misery one simpering, heavy-lidded head at a time.

I'd like to say that there's a little Jack of Clubs in all of us, but I can't make good on that. Me? Yes, there's plenty of the wretched little princeling in me, and it is from this wellspring of recognition that my loathing—*self*-loathing to name it properly—flows. You, I'm not so sure about. You may be the Jack of Diamonds, Spades, or Hearts, through and through. Mayhap you are a King or a Queen.

But I, a born wussie, I trump no one.

11. *Great Wussies I Have Known, Vol. 1*

A Tale of Two English Teachers

I have already belabored the obvious point that gayness and wussitude are entirely distinct phenomena (See Chapter 3). Yet if further proof be needed, then allow me to pass along the living object lesson team-taught by our high school English teacher/drama coach Mr. Carver and his successor, Mr. Black.

You see, this wussie/gay distinction was far from obvious in the Mortonville of my youth, a community of white-skinned red-staters nestled in the gold-green heart of Illinois corn country. Hard-nosed Dutch farmers and merchants had settled the area, so that one of our major entertainments every year was watching the teachers new to our district hack their way through class rosters clogged with Heusinkvelds, Van Couvenhovens and Quacken-bosches.* Our high school principal had been Ronald Reagan's college roommate and was proud of it. Perhaps one starts to get

---

* Since becoming a teacher who works in an alien culture myself, I've developed some retroactive sympathy for those outsiders. I mean, there you are, making your best effort to inject some semblance of dignity into the name "Beverdijk" only to have its humorless possessor insist on being called "Beaver-dyke." Around that point in the roll call you realize that you're never making it to Zuyderwyk alive.

the picture. It was a place where any teenage male's ineptitude at sports or long-standing lack of a female companion raised eyebrows.

Meanwhile, Mr. Carver, sophomore English teacher and drama coach, was a homosexual. Mortonville didn't ask and Mr. Carver didn't tell, which was just as well: The town wouldn't have known how to process the information. He wore crisply pressed slacks that accentuated his remarkably narrow butt. The tightness of these slacks contrasted with his shirts, which were billowy, almost blouse-like, and shiny, and of assorted colors, mostly pastels— though there was a grape Kool-Aid-hued one in the mix that he set off with a canary-yellow necktie, always perfectly knotted over an Adam's apple that actually was the size of a small green apple.

His short, receding chestnut hair occasionally and abruptly turned iridescent orange, a phenomenon that short-circuited the town's limited deductive prowess. *It's almost as if he dyes it,* people mused in the privacy of their thoughts. *But...but that just can't be... Men don't dye their hair...*

All in all it was a remarkable fashion statement for that time and place. No other male teacher would have known where to find a grape Kool-aid-hued dress shirt and certainly wouldn't have worn such a garment to school, not just because it wasn't done but because of the sweat stains that would spread from the armpits and back as a day of yelling and arm-flapping dragged on. No problem for Mr. Carver. He seldom yelled and never sweated.

He brought to his classes an attitude of such sneering condescension, conveyed through his trademark nasal whine, that chronic troublemakers didn't know what to make of him. Boys who normally competed to see who could be the biggest asshole in the room found themselves preempted by him, for dainty little *Monsieur Carvaire*—all five-foot-five of him—instantly became the biggest asshole in any room he deigned to bustle into.

He earned the nickname by competently reciting some French phrases that popped up in a short story one day during a sophomore English class that some of my lunch-mates attended.

Eww, Monsieur! Monsieur Car-VAIRE! they had heckled. *Mon Dieu!* Such *savoir faire! Bon jour! Sacre bleu!* they gabbled on and on, tossing in whatever faux French they could muster. *Eau de cologne! Pepe Le Pew!*

Monsieur Carvaire took this in the proper spirit, even coaching his antagonists so that they could mock him more accurately, for he had the knack, so rare in high school teachers, of distinguishing laughed-with from laughed-at. "Mish-*yoo!* It's mish-*yoo,* Mr. Temboer," he mewled at a right tackle who had addressed him as Mansewer.

—□—

Most of these suddenly Francophone friends of mine, it should be noted, were ardent homophobes back then and perhaps still are today, but they had fallen under the spell of the enigmatic Monsieur Carvaire, and would bring envy-inducing reports of his latest antics to our lunch table almost daily. While no quintessence of enlightened thought re sexual preference myself, I came to know him as director of the one-act play he cast me in.

Perhaps supposing that he had not yet given the good townsfolk sufficient opportunity to discern his orientation, the good Monsieur selected for his production "The Valiant," a talky piece set in a men's prison. Jeff Woodman and I took the two leads, a condemned prisoner and the warden who invites him into his office for thirty minutes of metaphysical pre-electrocution chitchat. He ran, as the saying goes, a tight ship: we would be punctual; we would memorize our lines at once; we would follow instructions. We tried to smuggle adlibs into the dialogue but Monsieur was too sharp for us. "Cut the crap," he would snap, and we did. As was said of King Lear, he had that in his countenance which I would fain call master.

By the end of the play the prisoner has won the warden's admiration but not a stay of execution. As the guard and I escorted the prisoner off stage to his present doom, I paused and raised my hands in front of my agonized face to convey the tragic irony of my powerlessness. "Cut the crap," barked Monsieur. I pleaded with him until he let me keep the bit, but only at the price of having to hear a long nasal sigh every time I did it, even in performance.

— ¤ —

All of us in the production yearned to work with him again, but it was not to be. At the end of that year's contract the good Monsieur set out in search of a place that came closer to meeting his aesthetic standards. In effect, he fired Mortonville. One of my friends had the great fortune to witness his departure. Evidently he could not bear to fold any of his clothes for packing, and so he had transformed his Volvo into a rolling closet. Suits and sweaters and blousy shirts were strung across the entire backseat and half of the front.

It was when Monsieur was exiting the post office that my friend spotted him. As he tried to reenter the car, he found that his shirts had fluffed out to the point that they now encroached on the driver's seat. After considerable wrangling with his wardrobe he managed to reclaim the minimal space necessary to start the engine and shift gears, after which he rolled out of that redneck prairie town swathed in a billowing pastel cloud of glory, never to return.

— ¤ —

Mr. Black inherited Monsieur Carvaire's classroom and schedule and extracurricular duties, but none of his panache. If just one word were to be used to describe him, that word would be *brittle*. If a second could be added, it would be *combustible*—not in the sense of having a short temper (though that was true enough), but in the sense of being easy to set on fire.

His dry, grayish hair sat upon his hatchety head like so much winter hay. His hollow, acne-scarred cheeks and wide eyes gave the impression that he was forever sucking on a dog-turd mint. His suits, made for a man of average breadth, shifted on his bony frame like a bag half-full of marbles. He was twenty-five going on eighty.

We first sampled his jumpy supervisory stylings in a study hall packed with unpronounceable VanWhatzits eager to test the new man's mettle. Mr. Black was equally determined to rule with an iron fist. He grasped instinctively that in order to win our respect he would have to challenge one of us to single combat and prevail, but had the misfortune to choose Shane Marshall as his opponent.

"Excuse me! Excuse me!" warbled Mr. Black halfway through an uneventful period. "Excuse me, you in the blue and white shirt?" But Shane, lost in thought and momentarily forgetting his color scheme for the day, continued gazing into the middle distance, forcing a flustered Mr. Black to refer to his seating chart.

"Shane Marshall, is it?"

"Yes?"

"Young man, can I help you with something?"

"I don't know. Can you?"

Shane Marshall was Mortonville High's Renaissance Man: all-conference running back, Honor Roll regular, blond and dapper scion of a wealthy North Side family, founding editor (with me and three others) of Mortonville High's underground newspaper, future attorney, and a preternaturally unflappable wiseass who had faced down many a seasoned faculty pro in the very sort of public dustup that Mr. Black now seemed to be spoiling for.

"Well, I'd just like to know," said Mr. Black, "why it is that you've been staring at me for the last three minutes."

"I wasn't staring at you."

"Well, what do you call what you're doing right now?"

"You're talking to me now. Wouldn't it be rude not to look at you?"

"Before, though. *Before!* You were staring right at me! *Don't you try to deny it.*"

"All right."

"All right *what?*"

"All right, I won't try to deny it if you tell me that I can't. But I would deny it if I could."

The entire population of the study hall awaited Mr. Black's comeback, which was a disappointing "Well…just *watch* it, mister! You hear me?"

Shane shrugged and poured his attention into a book. Mr. Black, who had been leaning forward with hands splayed on his desk, sat down and perused his seating chart, satisfied that his uncompromising stand had defused a tense situation. Time marched on.

When Mr. Black glanced back at Shane a minute later, he found his foe still engrossed in his book while a half dozen other students spaced about the cafeteria were now staring at him.

To no one in particular he inquired, "Now—now just what is going on here?" and got no response. "Just stop it! Stop it right now! You! You there in the tee-shirt! Stop staring at me!"

"But you're talking to me now," droned a junior boy, staring at him.

The rest of the period was a steep, downward spiral for Mr. Black and proved, if further proof were needed, that authority will last in the hands of a wussie about as long as lunch money.

—□—

In his role as drama coach, Mr. Black was placed in command of that fall's Junior Class Play. He chose that old chestnut *Our Town*, lured no doubt by the simplicity of its famous bare stage.

He must have forgotten, though, that in stark contrast to "The Valiant," a two-man show for the most part, *Our Town* entailed a large ensemble cast—a cast flush with students who had witnessed or read in the paper of his ignominious thrashing in the Study Hall Staredown. He did himself no favors by casting me in the minor role of Mr. Webb after I had lobbied for the lead, either. Heck hath no fury like a wussie scorned.

To say the least, *Our Town* would be a turbulent production. Most of the cast were first-timers who refused to memorize lines. They wrote them down instead on scrap paper, on sleeves, on props, on each other. I did memorize mine, but only so that I could start riffing on them, which started a trend.

"Stop changing your lines, Mr. Webb!" Mr. Black would squeak from the blackness of the auditorium.

Memorize your lines!
Don't miss your cue!
Speak louder!
Stop fiddling with the thunder machine!

Mr. Black's commands invariably had either no effect or the opposite of their desired one. The thunder "machine," for example, was nothing more than a wide sheet of metal hung from a rope backstage that had attracted no interest until Mr. Black called our attention to it, after which it could not have acquired more allure had it been festooned with *Playboy* fold-outs.

If I had possessed Mr. Black's remarkable power to always be contradicted, I would have barked things like "Do *not* spray gasoline all over each other and then ignite it!" or "Keep breathing!" Fortunately for us, he never learned to harness his gift.

Meanwhile, in the role of Simon Stimson, the embittered, ineffectual, gossiped-about conductor of a Grover's Corners church choir who ultimately hangs himself in an attic, Zach Geingob appeared to be doing something of a Mr. Black impersonation. Nothing in Zach's history suggested he was capable of such subversion, though, so it may have been coincidental. In those years, one could assume, legions of semi-competent high school actors playing Simon Stimsons in *Our Town* productions across the nation were doing spot-on Mr. Black imitations without knowing it.

—◻—

The reader, I suspect, now anticipates some amusing tale about our public performance, but alas, there is no such thing to tell. Halfway through rehearsals the revelation that we could end up looking like a pack of jackasses in front of the community settled in, forcing us to sober up. It's true that the *Our Town* that we performed bore only superficial similarities to the Pulitzer Prize-winning play conceived by Thornton Wilder, but it was well received by the audience of parents and grandparents and younger siblings nonetheless. Mr. Black had managed to weld the usual motley assortment of geeks, wussies, closeted gays and divas into a cohesive force—not by commanding our respect, but by uniting us in our indifference to him.

It occurs to me far too late into this little sketch, the entire point of which was to contrast the tough, gay teacher with the straight, wussie one, that I can summon forth no evidence of the unwed Mr. Black's heterosexuality. His appetites were, to us his students, as imponderable as they were uninteresting. All I can do is to state the obvious—that the odds favored his being attracted to females; and really, even if Mr. Black had tried to come out gay, those of us who remembered his steely predecessor would have pooh-poohed the claim. "We knew the homo English teacher," we would have told him. "We worked with the homo English teacher. The homo English teacher was a friend of ours. Mr. Black, you're no homo English teacher."

Ultimately, the flamboyant mantle of Monsieur Carvaire proved too heavy for Mr. Black to shoulder. Toward the end of his lone academic year at Mortonville High, I attended a party for drama club students held at the home of Mr. and Mrs. Battersby, the leading lights of Mortonville High theater, and it was here that I last laid eyes on Mr. Black.

He was in the kitchen, which the faculty in attendance had staked out as a student-free zone, perched atop a high stool like an old-fashioned dunce and holding his veiny, blade-like head in one hand and a large amber drink in the other. I couldn't hear what he was saying, but Mrs. Battersby was patting his shoulder in a consolatory way as he delivered some lengthy soliloquy.

His doppelganger Simon Stimson finishes his part in the play as a ghost rattling around in the Grover's Corners cemetery who derides human existence as nothing but "ignorance and blindness":

Yes, now you know! Now you know! That's what it was to be alive. To move about in a cloud of ignorance; to go up and down trampling on the feelings of those about you. To be always at the mercy of one self-centered passion or another!

So maybe Mr. Black was spiraling into that mode at the party when Mrs. Battersby slowly closed the kitchen door to give him some privacy, lest he once again overreact to staring eyes. He had been sent to us ripe for breaking and was leaving us thoroughly broken.

12. *Profiles in Wussitude, Vol. 3*

The Self-Evident Wussie

Part 1: A Twenty-First Century Wussie's Open Letter to Thomas Jefferson

Dear Thomas:

I'm sorry to disturb your eternal slumber like this. God knows you've earned it. I'd have written sooner, but the awkward truth of it is that you passed away a hundred and thirty-some Fourths of July before I was old enough to compose so much as a thank-you note to my grandmother. I must, perforce, beg your pardon for my tardiness.

My intentions, I assure you, are the noblest. Here in the twenty-first century, I regret to inform you, your reputation has been hijacked by an unseemly element. Blackguards. Hectors. Bullies. You know—Hamilton types. They would recast you in the eyes of our children—yes, our innocent little pledges—as some sort of bullnecked superhero, a principled and valiant bulwark against tyranny who didn't so much write the Declaration of Independence as quarry it.

It thus falls upon us, a small and silly band of Yankee Doodles who have actually skimmed your entire Wikipedia page, to preserve, protect, and defend your proper status as the Original American Wussie. It is an office, sir, that I execute with pride.

Look: I can't honestly say that I've always been a big fan. You and I got off to a rocky start when my social studies teacher made our class memorize the first two graphs of the Declaration and we eighth-graders crashed headlong into your serpentine Enlightenment syntax. Frankly, sir, I hated you for about a week— you and your damned dashes—until I realized my error of transference and figured out who the real enemy was pursuit-of-happiness-wise. I'm pretty sure you had someone a lot like Mrs. McGunnell in mind when you hauled off and made that crack about the blood of tyrants watering the tree of liberty.

In college during the Seventies (the Nineteen Seventies, let me clarify), my classmates and I rediscovered you on our own terms. I mean, the ponytail, the padding about the White House in your muddy gardening clothes, the revolutionary trash-talk—you had us at *We hold these truths*, dude. (And I use that term affectionately. For my generation, you were precisely the sort meant to be called, by dudes, "dude," dude.) Our college was in rural southern Minnesota (northern Louisiana Purchase to you. And thanks a load for that, by the way. Growing up speaking French might have queered my career as an English teacher.), so your whole agrarian motif went over really big around there, too.

In fact, we dearly wanted to feel a more personal connection to you, but that didn't come easily. We had grown up knowing you mainly from statuary, from your profile on the nickel, from nearby Mount Rushmore, etc. In a carved medium, you come off like just the sort of semi-divine man-mountain that today's naughty revisionists want to make of you. We could almost picture you and Washington as tag-team partners at a colonial WrestleMania: "And in this corner, in the star-spangled trunks...*the Slaaaaaaaave Drivers!!*"

Gradually, though, we acquired some sense of what it might have been like to hang with you—the authentic you. (Forget what Franklin said about hanging together or hanging separately. The term is benign.) You were a tall fellow for your day, six foot and then some, but darn near anorexic. Sure, you could tear the Williamsburg phone book in half, but only because no one yet had a phone.

You were no pro wrestler, if for no other reason than that the job requires a lot of loud and aggressive opining in public, something you quite frankly sucked at. (And by the way, just how the heck did you pull off successful careers in law *and* politics with that handicap?) Anyway, in the WWE, you wouldn't even have lasted as a manager—which, of course, is all to your credit.

Painters caught the real you better than sculptors did, I'd like to think. I especially like the Charles Willson Peale portrait. Remember that one? It was back in '91, your State Department days. You come off as a composite of all the companions in Oz. The eyes convey that sad, hard-earned knowledge of a scarecrow that's been set ablaze more than once in recent memory, while the rest of the face looks as rusted and pinched and weary as a tin man's. That reddish-gray mane, of course, belongs to the Cowardly

Lion. Dorothy gave you that sense of forever longing to get back home. Somewhere in there lurks Toto, too. Sir, you have no idea what I'm talking about, do you.

Anyhow, it was that portrait that grabbed me later in life—that finally let me see you for what you are. The Mrs. McGunnells of the land need a granite icon, a fearless and upright and muscular Apollo for their Revolutionary pantheon, but we, your fellow wussies, know the real you. You're one of us, Thomas, and we're not going to give you up without a fight. *With* a fight, of course, we'd give you up at once. We're wussies!

—□—

This is apt to stir up no small reaction among the Mrs. McGunnells of the land, Thomas, some of whom have their own daily radio programs these days. *Now, hold on there a minute*, they will sputter, *just hold your horses. Thomas Jefferson? The Thomas Jefferson? He of the Jefferson Memorial, of Mount Rushmore, of the nickel and the two-dollar bill? Okay, forget the two-dollar bill, but still: THE Thomas Jefferson? Of the Lewis and Clark Expedition and the University of Virginia? The guy who not only signed the Declaration of Independence, but who wrote the thing to boot? The guy who came up with the whole idea of pledging lives, fortunes, and sacred honor? Him you're calling a wussie? Oh, really?*

That's what the talk radio hosts will say, Thomas. You know the type. Just think Patrick Henry on steroids. Okay, forget the "on steroids"—that cliché wore out its welcome three presidents ago. My point is, this is what things have come to: the Patrick Henrys of our day have become your "defenders."

Now, if you or I only had the nerve, we could remind those blowhards that writing the Declaration wasn't your idea in the first place, that you only did it to get Adams and Franklin off your back. (And that swarthy little Adams—talk about a monkey on one's back!) Moreover, that signature of yours—small, faint, abbreviated, and buried near the bottom of the middle column—doesn't exactly shimmer with pride of authorship. ("Th. Jefferson"? Were you planning to sic the British on some unsuspecting Theo or Thad in the next county?)

On the whole, you seemed more than happy to let King George assume that the whole thing sprang from the hand of that sluggard Hancock. Not that you weren't happy to claim sole authorship of it on your tombstone, once the prospect of any nasty drawing or quartering or bad reviews had been removed. A classic wussie move, Thomas, and I mean that in the most adoring way.

To be sure, you did tack on that nifty syncopated flourish about pledging lives, fortunes and sacred honor, and did so when there was a strong possibility that the British would prevail in the war, that they would track down every signatory one by one—no doubt rounding up every poor Th. Jefferson they could get their mitts on just to be sure—and would extract said lives, fortunes, and honor in excruciating ways. Hey, I subsisted on their food for three solid months during my quarter abroad in London, so believe you me, I know what torments and depredations those people are capable of.

I suppose, then, that you may not have blossomed into full wussihood by the time of the Revolution. You may have started out in life with the emotional strength of an oak until time and misfortune whittled you down to an easily bent sapling—or a willow, as Abigail Adams once called you. (Oops... Maybe you weren't aware of that characterization. Sorry, sir: the only smoking shorty among the revolutionary elite totally called you a willow. For what it's worth, I think she meant it as a compliment.)

Forgive the painful recap of your formative years, but: You lost your father, your best friend, your favorite sister—and Fate was just getting warmed up on your bony white ass because after that, it was to be your wife and eventually four of your five daughters.

I once suffered a complete mental collapse after someone broke up with me. No, seriously. Meanwhile, you muddled your way through all of the above taking solitary horseback rides and writing out meditations on the nature of Grief. So I have to give you a tip of the three-cornered hat for your far vaster reserves of emotional strength.

But over time, blow by blow, insult by insult, I think those reserves were depleted, and as a result you became less and less resilient, less and less optimistic. More and more willowish. More and more like us.

Some men are born wussies, some achieve wussitude, and some have wussitude thrust upon them. I'm Column A and you're Column C. But at the end of the day, we're both wussies. And you can count on me to tirelessly remind our fellow Americans of that fact until such time as, you know, one of them yells at me or something.

Looking forward to your reply,

> I have the honor of remaining your Most
> Humble Servant and brother in Wussitude,

> Josh Muggins

Part 2: What an Asshole, Eh?

Having posted my fawning letter to Jefferson, I suppose the most fitting tribute I could now make to the man would be a thorough trashing of him behind his back, since that is what Jefferson himself—equal parts weenie and wussie—was wont to do after posting fawning letters to people. After all, this was a chap who:

➤ Sucked up to Patrick Henry for years while confiding to others that the rebel icon was "avaritious & rotten hearted" and "without logic, without arrangement," finally telling Madison, "What we have to do is devoutly pray for his death."

➤ Similarly backstabbed Washington, Adams, the French...

➤ Did manage to maintain one enduring friendship based on mutual affection and respect—with Madison—until suddenly feeling compelled to blab to someone on his deathbed how "He could never in his life stand up against strenuous opposition"—effectively calling *Madison* a wussie.

➤ Denounced slavery as an abomination in a book written in his youth for foreign consumption, then did everything he could to keep the tome from falling into the hands of his slaveholding neighbors.

But such unseemly episodes are best set aside for this book's sequel, *Weenie: In Praise of Faithless Men.* Our emphasis here is on the more endearing wussie aspect of Jefferson's persona, and for this, too, there is no shortage of examples; for when Jefferson wasn't busy sniping and carping, he was busy ducking and covering. Or, to couch it in his own idiom:

The history of Thomas Jefferson is a history of repeated skedaddles and retreats, all having in direct object the preservation of his own hide and reputation. To prove this, let facts be submitted to a candid world.

➤ In 1774, barely in his thirties, he boldly wrote up a list of instructions for his Virginia elders (Washington, Henry, et al) to lug up to the Continental Congress. Then he called in sick on the day he could have presented those very views in person to those very bigwigs. But meddling friends had the thing published in pamphlet form with his name on it, and before he knew it he had a seat at the big table in Philadelphia...

➤ ...where he uttered scarcely a peep for months, sulked visibly while his Declaration was "mangled" by committee, * denounced the official version (stealthily, of course), produced his own Director's Cut of the thing, and then went back to sulking through the rest of '76.

➤ As governor of Virginia during the Revolutionary War, he ran away from British troops as they advanced on Monticello. Cooler heads forgave him that, but even the coolest were apt to turn on him when, his term in office having conveniently expired in the middle of the siege, he simply walked off the job like an Olive Garden server abandoning a table of obstreperous under-tippers to the busboy at the end of a shift.

➤ Later, as Secretary of State, he would bring inadvertent delight to generations of unborn male social studies students by noting that "Hamilton and myself were daily pitted in the cabinet like two cocks." But more to the point for our purposes, he let the runty Hamilton run circles around him until he picked up his toys and moved back to Monticello in a snit...only to be dragged out of his snit and back to the capital four years later when he was elected Adams's vice president...

---

* Most painful for Jefferson was the excision of his attempt to blame King George III of all people for foisting slavery upon innocently bystanding colonial slaveholders like himself—though whether that counts as a wussie move or a towering act of weenitude, I can't quite figure out. Franklin, who understood the pain of being edited better than most, tried to mollify Jefferson with one of his patented longwinded, had-to-be-there anecdotes—something about the evolution of a sign for a certain hat shop—but alas, to no avail.

➢ …after which he tucked tail and skulked back to Monticello yet *again.*

➢ Long story short, when he wasn't busy being driven back to Monticello, he was being driven away from there. In post-presidential retirement he was yet again forced *out* of the Monticello house by an invading horde—this time of adoring tourists.

A more imposing statesman (think Washington) would have sent the rabble scurrying for cover with a booming "Now, see here, you people!" A more enterprising one (think Franklin) would have charged them admission. Jefferson's response was to let people wander the grounds and feed at his table while he hid out at a second estate, leaving his family and his slaves (pretty much one and the same by that time) to entertain the huddled masses yearning to eat free—and thereby aggravating the humongous debts he was already preparing to saddle those very heirs with.

➢ On those rare occasions when he could enjoy a quiet meal at home unmolested, he drank wine—wine by the thimbleful, diluted with water. Yes, while the real he-men of the revolution hoisted steins of rich, foamy American beer in Boston taverns to lube themselves up for long nights raiding ships in the harbor or getting heroically massacred on icy streets, Jefferson sipped imported, diluted wine.

One of those tough mooks in Boston, Sam Adams, got a beer company named after his bad self. I bought their stock; then it tanked. But that's neither here nor there. The point is, nobody names their brand for a serial sipper and diluter. Instead, you get dumped onto the two-dollar bill.

—◻—

Now that's what you could call a wussie life, fully lived: one that merits a plaque mounted alongside those of Isaac and Hirohito.

Except for one thing. Wussie purists seeking to deny Jefferson admission to our pantheon can always point to one flaw, the one wussie credential that he glaringly lacked: i.e., a spectacular ineptitude in mating. For, whereas those other two illustrious wussies never would have come within field-goal range of an exposed vagina without concerned elders acting as Sherpas (after which both still had a devil of a time mastering the whole baby-making mechanism) neither Jefferson nor his sperm was shy with the ladies.

From the time he first arrived at college from the provinces, he was popular at the balls—though one ought not to read too much into that. These raves were eighteenth-century affairs at the College of William and Mary, after all, so the girls had chaperones, who in turn had chaperones of their own. Plus the girls wore foundation garments, which in turn wore foundation garments of their own. What with all the fasteners and hoops and corsets and trip-wires and buried mines that a fellow had to navigate to get to the goods, it's no wonder Jefferson later became so obsessed with architecture.

But he found and charmed his bride all on his lonesome and merrily set about impregnating her as frequently as humanly possible. Pretty much impregnated her to death, or so some critics believe.

Anyway, she died, and he was sent off to pre-Revolutionary Paris, where even a Franklin-stove-shaped Franklin was rumored to still be running up some pretty good innings well into his codgerhood. In France, the rather dweebish Jefferson wasn't getting around nearly as much as tongue-cluckers like the frustrated, incessantly masturbating Adams assumed that he was. He did, however, famously hook up for a time with some other dude's wife.

Indeed, throughout the Fall of '86, whenever he wasn't with Maria Cosway, he was writing letters to her—up to four thousand words a pop—or else writing letters to others about her; and, tellingly, he never backstabbed her too egregiously. Still, smart money says that even the Cosway Infatuation was more smoke than fire.*

However, hot on the heels of Mrs. Cosway came a certain pretty slave girl…

—◻—

Oh dear, now I have gone and done it. I have invoked the "pretty slave girl." In so doing, I have roused the sleeping giant. I have drawn Mrs. McGunnell wild out of her grave. The dry, dusty throat of the self-proclaimed defenders of Jefferson's legacy now finds its collective voice.

And for my part, I do not shy away from a debate with these guardians of Jefferson's supposed Christ-like virtue. Indeed, I welcome that debate, just so long as we hold it here in my book, over which I retain complete editorial control. So lay on, Macduff, and all that.

As I was saying, then, along came a certain pretty little slave girl…

…at which the Voice of the Guardians is all, like: *Now, hold on a minute. Just hold on!*… And then, after coughing up a clot of phlegm: *That Sally Hemings business—that's all speculation!*

---

* Of course you won't be satisfied with vague incendiary metaphors, will you. You need the nitty-gritty: *Did they do it, or not?*

Well, I tell you: Screenwriters want to say no, historians tend to say yes. I'll split the difference and say handjobs.

Handjobs gibe with Mrs. Cosway's stated desire to avoid pregnancy at all costs, and they could easily have pulled it off (pardon the expression) on any number of long carriage rides along the Seine.

What, you don't think they had handjobs in the 1700s? This was France, remember. And I'm telling you, no man, no matter how stupendous a wussie, churns out that much fruity correspondence without some sort of tactile reinforcement. I know whereof I speak.

To which I, speaking for all who hold dear the more human and fallible wussie-weenie concept of Jefferson, reply: Well, yes. Absolutely. Except that it isn't. The 1996 DNA tests were a slam dunk. They even excluded Jefferson's nephews. Then there's the Hemings family's oral history to consider.

Yeah, sure, but…

Oh, and the recently discovered log book in Jefferson's own handwriting, documenting the duration and positions and degree of satisfaction for every instance of unprotected intercourse that occurred between him and Sally over three decades.

Aw…crap.

Okay, I made up the log book. But you guys bought that awfully easily.

Well, the whole thing is just so…so unseemly. One of the Founding Fathers, the author of the Declaration, for heaven's sake, skulking off to a filthy slave cabin in the dead of night like those guys in Roots—*you know, Lou Grant and Pa Walton and Chuck Connors and all them…*

Far be it from me to make light of the whole vile business of people owning other people. But for what it's worth, there probably was no slave cabin in this scenario and Jefferson was certainly no Chuck Connors. Sally and her siblings were house servants and artisans. No field work, no lashes. Sally's day job evidently consisted of tending to clothes, helping with babies or with the sick and such.

That's all well and good, but still: There's the whole race-mixing aspect of the thing.

The word you're looking for, I think, is "miscegenation." A nasty word, *miscegenation*, and not a critter that you want to tangle with in the early rounds of a spelling bee, I want to tell you. If it makes you feel better, Sally had three Caucasian grandparents.

Backing up for just a second, Jefferson inherited the whole Hemings clan from his father-in-law, who, by the way, had taken Sally's mother as *his* companion during his own widowhood. So Sally was in fact the younger half-sister of Jefferson's late wife!

So…you're saying she was a white chick?

No one knows exactly, but put it this way. Suppose you visited your online adult entertainment provider and went to the "Interracial" section. (It occurs to me all too late now that I neglected to thank Thomas in my letter on behalf of all twenty-first century wussies for supporting the First Amendment.) Let's just say that if you downloaded the Sally/T-Jeff sex tape with sweaty anticipation of some hot Mandingo action, you would probably be disappointed.

Hmm… I do like the Interracial category… But still, when all is said and done, it's slavery, for God's sake. She's his property! It's coercive sex!

Ah, my made-of-straw friends, you're still going on this erroneous assumption that Jefferson was capable of coercing anyone to do anything. You might be interested to know that the Sally/T-Jeff affair started up during her time on his household staff in Paris, where slavery wasn't recognized—a fact that Sally surely soon discovered (no thanks to Jefferson, who was, let us not forget, also a practicing weenie). On any business day she might have strolled over to the Parisian Admiralty Court to petition for her freedom as other slaves did, but she elected not to.

What? Why the heck not?

Well, like a lot of wussies, T-Jeff had a knack for getting women to feel sorry for him. Henry Adams noted that "[H]is yearning for sympathy was almost feminine." You're talking about a guy who was powerful, yes, and persuasive, but also needy, which appeals to certain females. Or so I hear.

And he'd be something of a trophy, no? I was reading in the papers not long ago about this fellow who managed to attract just a whole slew of vivacious and engaging female companions on no more basis than his success in a number of golfing competitions. So just think of the value the writer of our one and only Declaration of Independence could command in the market.

So, everything was copacetic? They were both, like, into each other?

Evidently so. Jefferson immediately set about impregnating Sally at the same torrid pace he had maintained with his late wife— and this some two hundred years pre-Viagra! It appears they granted each other exclusive drilling rights from that day forward.

Then, why didn't he just free her and marry her? Didn't people do that?

Your ordinary, non-celebrity slaveholder did, sure. But it was a little dicier for a man shouldering both national political ambitions and as assload of wussitude, even if he could never quite fully admit to either. Near as we can figure, Sally browbeat Jefferson into agreeing to raise their children properly, arm them with useful skills, and then set them all free at adulthood—and she kept him to that. But freedom for Sally herself would have been problematic, especially after the scandal broke.

Huh? The scandal broke? During their lifetimes?

You bet it did—just as his campaign for reelection as president was heating up. Soon the press was all up in T-Jeff's shit, as it were, with satirical poems about "Dusky Sal" and "Black Sal." That human spittoon John Quincy Adams wrote some of them—anonymously, of course. (Those Adamses could have benefited from a few scoops of wussitude to take the edge off their vast weenitude, I tell you.) Jefferson denied everything, needless to say, but made no effort to hide Sally away—and stayed in the race.

That's awfully brazen. You've got to admit, it certainly doesn't smack of wussitude.

I'd score it half wussie, half weenie. He'd deny Sally's existence all week long in Washington, then ride home for the weekend and impregnate her again. Well, those two crazy kids made it work somehow.

But the American people were cool with it? They reelected him?

You'd certainly think that getting caught in an affair with a slave would hurt in the swing states, wouldn't you? I mean, it's at least as bad as invading a sovereign Middle Eastern nation for trumped-up reasons or getting hugged on TV by Sammy Davis, Jr. But when you've doubled the size of your country without firing a shot, Americans will cut you some slack—so yes, he won in a landslide. It helps, too, if your opponent is some guy named Pinckney.

"Pinckney"—hee-hee! You know, once you wrap your mind around the slavery thing and the dead-wife's-half-sister thing, the whole story really isn't all that despicable.

126

Even kind of romantic, eh?

Well…yeah. Yes, indeed! You know, the scales have fallen from my eyes! I was wrong to deny the evidence. The whole thing really makes a person think more, not less of Jefferson.

Great! Then again, there's that unfortunate business of him being in his forties and her being sixteen when he first knocked her up.

What? What was that? Did you say sixty—

Six*teen*. And him well into his forties.

What the— Huh? Six— Why, I— What the hell was wrong with that pasty-faced freak?

You'll have to ask Jefferson. I'm guessing it'll turn out King George was somehow to blame.

13. One Wussie's Obsession with Naked Ladies: Five Increasingly Disturbing Anecdotes

1. Early Stirrings

Once upon a time I had a thing for women twice my age. Around the age of seven, I began looking upon my adolescent cousins with lust—or with something akin to it—and was capable of acting on my desires with remarkably unwussie-like flamboyance.

My cousin Phil, three years my senior but younger than his three blonde sisters, confided to me that on various occasions and through no fault of his own he had seen each of them naked. I loathed him for the matter-of-fact way that he delivered this news as we flipped through *Archie* comics in his bedroom. Envy rolled over me like molten wax, searing my soul—yes, my very soul.

A few summers later, cousin Amy unilaterally reached the decision that it was time for me to learn to swim properly. There I was, a carefree nine-year-old, dog-paddling my way around the shallow end of the Goosens' pool, when without warning I fell into the clutches of this lithe, nurturing eighth-grader.

Amy supported me at the waterline with her arms thrust under my chest and groin like the tines of a forklift as our mothers beamed approvingly from poolside through congruent red-framed cat's-eye sunglasses. I repeatedly rebuffed Amy's condescending entreaties that I practice the crawl stroke in this undignified pose. "It's all right; I won't let you go under," she cooed. Finally, I grabbed her swimsuit top between the cups and tried to yank it off.

I knew it was a despicable thing to do even as I did it, but in what I must say was a rather precocious display of logic for a grade-schooler I reasoned that there was no real downside. Of my two objectives—to see Amy's nipples and to end the swimming lesson—I was absolutely certain to attain at least one. And that is precisely what happened.

—◻—

My earliest sexual fantasy consisted of an endlessly looped scene in which two sitcom actresses, Mary Tyler Moore and Inger Stevens, engaged in a topless swordfight. Why those two, I don't know. As Woody Allen would later famously explain, the heart wants what it wants.

To my credit, I think, I tried not to have a fantasy life of any sort. I figured there had to be a Commandment against such thoughts, since there were Commandments for such mundane and less exciting sins as lying and saying goddam. So before allowing myself to imagine the swordfight every night, I had to pray, and pray hard. This was the clenched-teeth, balled-fisted praying of a true-believing eight-year-old Presbyterian. I prayed not for wisdom or forgiveness or super-strength or a life-sized Robot Commando, but rather for God to get His All-seeing Ass out of my pre-pubescent head for a half hour or so, so that I could think about topless swordfighting sitcom starlets free of His mood-dampening glare.

Of course I didn't put it that way in the prayer. I was a seriously flawed boy to be having such thoughts, I conceded to God right up front, and this would absolutely be the last time I asked Him for this, um, exception—*indulgence*, I suppose, was the word I was grasping for—but could He see His way clear to deal with some other business for just a little while? Surely His plate must be full.

I would give Him a minute to mull this proposal over and then—on the assumption that He was cool with it and had quietly hovered away—off came the tops and out came the swords.

The swords were actually fencing foils. Let me be clear about that. And they must have had proper safety tips because no blood was ever drawn. No, there was no sadism in the sexual fantasies of my childhood. I suspect the fencing was just a device to ensure plenty of hopping and bouncing, because at that age I simply didn't know what else to do with full-grown sitcom starlets once I had them topless.

The fights took place on a mysterious white expanse shrouded in mist that might have been Heaven or a set from *The Lawrence Welk Show*. And it was important to me that the combatants be the actresses themselves, not "Laura Petrie" and "Katy Holstrum." This device freed them from the romantic entanglements of their fictional counterparts (for not only was Laura married, but she had a son my age!). However, I gained no advantage from the women's supposed availability as I made no cameos in this fantasy. My perspective was very much a benign, omniscient one.

Both actresses wore tight dark slacks like those worn by Mary on *Dick Van Dyke*, and those slacks stayed put. I didn't want to deal with what lurked beneath them. Oh, let me shun that; that way madness lies.

Eventually, Inger would tap Mary on the sternum with her foil (or vice versa) to conclude the bout and I sailed off to dreamland, more or less at peace with my oddly acquiescent Lord.

2. Father Knows Best, Exhibit A

I relate these early examples of my boob fetish without shame. After all, *every* young boy has a boob fetish. Nothing remotely remarkable or reprehensible about that. It's a part of growing up. I will bet you that even Michael Jackson went through such a phase when he was a pre-teen, his fantasies no doubt entailing a couple of swordfighting Supremes.

But as your non-wussies mature and start having demystifying encounters with various sets of real-life boobs, boob fetishism inevitably retreats and gives way to more complex and grown-up fetishisms. Meanwhile, we wussies in middle and old age remain trapped in the mindset of a sexually confused eleven-year-old Motown phenom. It's a wonder we don't all whittle our noses down and cavort with chimpanzees.

I blame my parents. It was they, you see, who introduced me to soft-core pornography.

— ❑ —

That may be an actionable accusation, so let me interject a brief description here of the Mugginses of Mortonville, Illinois. We were a fun-loving middle-American clan. We had board-game nights, enjoyed ping-pong in the basement, got our favorite treats on birthdays. When the budget allowed, we piled into the station wagon and headed west on jolly and memorable vacations.

But our fun was of the primmest, most straight-laced stripe. For example, you might be amazed—as my friend Penniman was—to learn that when the Mugginses gathered around the black-and-white TV in the basement rec room to watch *The Dick Van Dyke Show* together and someone let slip an audible fart, custom dictated that *no one comment on it or display any visible reaction.* "I couldn't live like that," Penniman shuddered when I confessed this to him. My father may have chosen to live and work in the secular world, but he raised his family in a manner befitting the grandson and nephew of prominent Episcopal clergymen. But for the coffee and cola and cigarettes and cocktail parties, we could have passed as Mormons.

Oh, and the movies, too. By the mid-Sixties, my brother and sister were in high school and too cool for family outings, so when my parents decided to drive over to Darlington to see a movie it became an activity for just the three of us. It would have been just the two of them if my mother had had her way. "I don't think you'll be interested in this movie," my mother would invariably say, thereby piquing a theretofore dormant curiosity. I had learned that the more my mother demurred, the more titillation I could expect.

The 007 romp *Thunderball* was a prime example. At two solid hours of Euro-babes in bikinis and folks shooting each other underwater with spear guns, it fell right into the wheelhouse of someone who had been lolling himself to sleep to visions of topless swordfighting sitcom starlets for a full third of his life. I thought it a masterpiece.

—◻—

A year later, my parents issued no such admonitions of my likely disinterest before bringing me along to see *Hawaii*. This one, they knew, was safe. This would be no James Bond boobfest, certainly. The ad campaign suggested a sweeping historical saga about earnest nineteenth-century missionaries; perhaps there would even be some educational value. It starred Julie Andrews, for heaven's sake. Mary Poppins!

But by the mid-Sixties the world was changing rapidly, and neither my parents nor the Motion Picture Association of America was keeping up. Forty-odd minutes into what was shaping up as indeed a very starchy epic about starchy white folks in starchy clothes spouting starchy dialogue came the scene in which the missionaries' ship finally sails within sight of Maui, at which moment dozens of native nymphs dropped what they were doing, as well as what they were wearing, to swim out and greet them.

Look! Whoa! That girl's naked! You can see her whole boobs! Not just the tops!

And there's another one!

And that girl, too!

This was not your James Bondesque, strategically-shadowed pseudo-nudity, either. This was *nude*-nudity! Boobs! Boobs everywhere! Bippity-boppiting and shilly-shallying the live-long day away! Firm, ripe, ethno-nymph boobs! And on and on and on they came in wave after undulating wave…

They're all different, I remember thinking, *like snowflakes.*

Seated between my mother and father, I turned to the latter, on my left. His back was tilted forward at an odd angle. His eyelids fluttered and his Adam's apple had embarked on some sort of autonomous exercise regimen. He looked as if he were very slowly being electrocuted.

I dared not speak but sent him a telepathic message:

Dad… Aren't you going to stop me from watching this?

There was a pause.

Leave me alone, I sensed him replying. *My gosh, look at that one.*

So it's okay, then? I persisted. *God won't punish us?*

He didn't get back to me right away on that one, either, perhaps distracted by the three robust nymphs now climbing up the side of the ship. Finally, I felt him say:

We didn't know, Josh. We didn't know there'd be bare…bare breasts in the movie. And because we didn't know, it's all right.

Still without eye contact he continued, surprisingly eloquent in his telepathic voice:

We shouldn't go looking for bare breasts, son. That's wrong. But these…these breasts are coincidental *breasts, don't you see? They're just— well, they're there. They're just* there. *It's what artists call "the found object." Nobody can blame us for…for making use of them.*

And on that note, he fell silent.

Okay, got it, I replied.

I did not seek a second opinion from my mother.

3. Father Knows Best, Exhibit B

I was thirteen on Christmas morning 1968, the day my father unwrapped the January '69 edition of *Playboy*. My father laughed, my sister giggled, my mother gasped "Oh, Daddy!" and then quickly added, "Keep that thing away from Josh!"

My father laughed that Christmas morning because the *Playboy* was a gag gift from a bawdy relative, and he was comfortable enough in his buttoned-down skin (the *Hawaii* incident notwithstanding) to take the joke. Much less at ease in my hormone-roiled skin, I blushed and balled up my fists upon hearing my mother's restraining order. For while I had certainly heard much about the fabled *Playboy* magazine, had glimpsed its cover on the top shelf of the liquor store where I purchased my Marvel comics, had digested third-hand rumors of huge secret collections curated by classmates' older brothers, I had yet to survey an issue's contents.

Now, without warning, a *Playboy* had somehow breached the Muggins threshold, and before I could even wrap my adolescent mind around the implications of that fact, measures were being taken to ensure that I would get no closer.

—◻—

What gifts I received that Christmas are long forgotten—indeed were banished from my mind the moment the *Playboy* flopped free of its candy-cane-print wrapping paper. It was as if someone had unleashed a wild jungle cat into our one-story ranch-style home: Not for an instant could its existence be forgotten, nor could I silence the voice that nagged, *What are you going to do about it?* Time froze. There would be no sleeping, no, nor eating or digesting—no diversions of any kind—until that thick tablet of forbidden delights had been pried open and its every glossy secret revealed.

Around noon, cousins and grandparents flooded the house. The holiday crowd worked both for me and against me. There were more people whose movements needed to be monitored; but all the males of the extended clan soon drifted to the TV room in the basement while the females congregated in the kitchen, leaving the living room unguarded.

The living room was just around the corner from the kitchen but I slipped back in undetected. There, on the coffee table, bathed in the pastel glow of the GE frosted bulbs, sat the *Playboy*.

It called to me. *Jossssssh*, it hissed, serpent-like, through its disappointingly demure cover—a giant rendition of the magazine's white rabbit-head trademark set against an off-white background, and nary a playmate to be seen. *Open me, Josssssssh. Opennnnnnnnnn meeeeeee.*

I reached for it and then…wussied out. If my mother were to come around the corner and catch me leafing through the thing, I would be shamed. If it were my sister, I would be mocked. If one of my hot cousins, I would be pitied: *Oh, my, there goes the little pervert again.*

Then, too, there was something just wrong about reading *Playboy* by Christmas-tree light, with Santa's head embedded in the silver star perched atop the tree. *He knows if you've been bad or good,* and all that rot. It didn't help that half of Santa's face had been burned off a few years earlier, giving him the demeanor of a jolly old escaped mental patient.

Finally I buried the thing under a *Good Housekeeping* and a *Life* and hoped that everyone would forget about it.

—¤—

The relatives went home; the tree was dragged to the curb; a new year dawned. Dad went back to work, my brother and sister headed back to college, and I finally cornered the jungle cat.

It was not to be a leisurely read even under these improved circumstances. I would skim the *Playboy* in snatches—so to speak—when I was sure my mother was down in the laundry room, always straining to catch the muffled thump of her feet on the carpeted stairs. At her approach, I re-buried the treasure, wiped my sweaty palms on my pants, and summoned the visage of Mrs. McGunnell, the social studies teacher—a natural-born erection-strangler who never let me down.

The January Playmate of the Month was named Leslie. She had short brown hair and stark tan lines around her boobs and butt. I wondered how she had managed to get a tan like that in winter. Her nipples looked like you could erase a whole page of algebra problems with one of them.

Apart from Leslie's spread, the main attraction of the issue was a retrospective of all twelve Playmates from the previous year. Paging through that was a bit much for a novice *Playboy* reader, like getting twelve shots of heroin on your first day as a junkie.

Of course, that's not the analogy that occurred to me at the time, at age thirteen. Back then I probably would have gone with "like drinking twelve milkshakes without a pause to recover from the brain freeze," which probably works better than the heroin analogy anyway, all said and done. One lady, the recent Miss December, had nipples that were about as big as her face. *Damn!*, I would have said had I been allowed to say "damn." *As big as her whole face!*

— ¤ —

After a while, I actually found time to leaf through the boobless sections of the magazine, which was enormous—more pages than our Social Studies textbook! *An interview with Lee Marvin...think I'll pass... Two personal remembrances of the late Robert Kennedy...How can he be "late"? He's dead!... Playboy's Party Jokes... Huh? I don't get it... All these articles, all these guys I never heard of... Henry Miller, Peter Matthiessen, William Sloane Coffin—now that's a cool name... P.G. Wodehouse—a funny name...*

After my first day back at junior high, I came home to find the living room straightened up and the entire stack of magazines gone. I panicked. Where had they put it? I looked everywhere I could think to look, then came to the conclusion that since it ostensibly belonged to my father, he must have stashed it somewhere.

By this time it was early evening and Dad was watching TV in the basement, so I took the opportunity to ransack his desk in the master bedroom, which he promptly caught me doing. He extracted a blubbering confession from me with no need for a Bad Cop. He clapped me on the shoulder and told me it was all right. "It's all right," he said, in fact.

But he didn't tell me where that *Playboy* was, and I never found out.

4. Silly Putty

This time it's the skinny Christian girl from the opposite end of the hall, planting her foot on the left-side bench to facilitate the toweling off of the underside of her bare left leg.

I'd not given her much thought till now. I had glimpsed her a few times, shortly after moving to the coed floor of the dorm, as she emerged from the room with the Jesus poster on the door— one of those earnest, caring, hypersensitive Jesuses with whom no mortal man can compete—and quickly written her off. Any pursuit of that type of girl would have amounted to casting one's seed upon hard ground, I felt certain.

But now it's as if I am seeing her in a whole new light—which I am, of course. I'm seeing her in the pale, golden light of the changing room adjacent to the communal showers. Actually, the light isn't so golden when one is standing *in* the changing room; it only takes on this warm, amber hue because of the sloppily puttied-over window through which I am currently ogling the blissfully ignorant-of-being-ogled Christian Girl.

Turns out that under all those tent-like sweaters of hers, Christian Girl's got it going on. I have to give it up for Christian Girl. Not right here on the spot, of course—for I am standing in the narrow entryway by which we access both the restroom and shower-room, and if someone shoves the door open and enters at a brisk pace, presumably in urgent need of the restroom facilities located off to the right, they will surely catch me squinting into the metal door to the left, i.e. the door to the changing room, and it won't take this hypothetical barger-inner long to figure out exactly why I'm there—or to figure out that the five-inch-square window in the door to the changing room, which was hastily puttied over when the floor went coed, bears the tiniest sliver of unputtied-over glass surface in the top right corner, through which an unscrupulous resident can observe his neighbors disrobing before a shower or toweling off afterward.

This being the case, I will tarry in this place just a wee bit longer until all the loose ends have been tied up and all my questions answered; then I'll skitter back to my room on wobbly legs, lock the door, and literally give it up for Christian Girl.

—□—

As I lie on my mattress in the aftermath of giving it up for Christian Girl, Shame, like a thief in the night, will come tiptoeing upon me. But then my internal bouncers will hustle Shame unceremoniously out the door, and I will quickly convince myself that no, no, *no*...

No, this is not my fault. It wasn't I who scraped off that little opening in the putty, after all. I don't know who it was. Maybe nobody scraped the putty off; maybe it was just one of those zany, serendipitous puttying mishaps that life heaves forth from time to time.

Besides, I towel off in that changing room myself, and Christian Girl is welcome to ogle me anytime she likes. Creep I may be, but no hypocrite!

No, the hole wasn't my fault. I had merely gone to do my business in toilet stall number four one day, after which, on my way out, the motion sensor in my peripheral vision—that same survival tool our ancestors thoughtfully evolved for eluding predatory mountain lions and which now, in our largely post-mountain lion epoch, serves modern man in a variety of ways including but by no means limited to the spotting of puttying mishaps—sent a giddy express synapse-o-gram to my visual cortex reading: *Naked neighbor at three o'clock!*

And what a naked neighbor that one was! Yes, I had hit the jackpot on that first turn of the lever. It was What's-her-name, the one who came to the kitchenette to fix her salad that one time when I was there frying a burger, the one with the forlorn Bambi eyes and the irksome propensity to drag the boyfriend-back-in-Hooterville into the conversation whether or not the topic merited his insertion.

And it's not as if I loiter in the hallway, waiting for a pretty girl to head for the showers, I reminded myself, aerobically rationalizing. *Now,* that *would be creepy.*

—◻—

I saw other naked neighbors during my single quarter at Searing Center—females, males, even one combo. I became an equal opportunity pervert, a deviant of catholic tastes. I can't honestly say that I feel guilty about it now as I look back, though certainly this cavalier attitude is largely a function of never having got caught in the act.

When one chances upon sights of ineffable natural beauty, one has a duty to stop and admire them. That was my ultimate rationalization.* There was a phrase for this phenomenon that echoed down to me from the dim, dark past: the Found Object.

And oh how those Found Objects would have a way of finding me down through the years. I might have contemplated obtaining a restraining order against Found Objects by the time I had lived in Japan for several years, as the last of these tales illustrates.

---

* Then again, I suppose my *ultimate* rationalization was "What if somebody slipped while toweling off and knocked herself unconscious? Isn't it our duty to check on each other? Isn't that what neighbors are for?"

5. Field Trip

The day of the annual field trip to the English reading room has come round again and, as per custom, I am leading a small group of advanced students of the Study Abroad Preparation Course here so that they can practice research skills in an English-language environment prior to departure for enrollment in various small colleges spread throughout the Great Satan.

Here—specifically, a small-scale model of an American library run by the U.S. Information Agency atop a downtown Tokyo office building—they can practice finding resources for the small-scale research projects that I have assigned them. Each member is to find one relevant book and one relevant periodical article—a sort of scholarly scavenger hunt, if you will. But an exception is made for Tadashi, along for the trip but not ready to begin a research project.

—◻—

Tadashi is exceptional in many ways. He joined the class a third of the way through the term, for one thing. For another, he has not uttered a word to me or to his classmates except when called upon to do so in class. For a third, he reportedly has already been to a college in the Great S., which would seem to disqualify him from enrollment in a Study Abroad "Preparation" Course. But I was told there was a rational explanation for this when he was brought to my class.

He was small and pale, with an inky Bert-on-Sesame-Street unibrow and all the *joie de vivre* of a slow-moving low front. He stared balefully at me without blinking as I tried to catch him up on the activities of my writing class, unnervingly refusing to interject "I see's" and "Uh-huh's" and such when custom called for them.

"And another thing you should do is keep an English journal in a notebook...You-you got that?... I collect them from everybody on Mondays…" (*For God's sake, say something.*) "Um, try to write at least 300 words…" (*Or at least stop staring.*) "Any topic is okay…" (*Seriously, just stop staring at me.*) "Some people write about their favorite musicians or movies, others write about trips they've taken…" (*Would you stop staring at me for five hundred yen?*) "When they don't have any other ideas, they just write about what they've been doing or thinking lately…" (*I'm going to explain the functions of the dash on Friday; may I use your unibrow as a model?…*) "Uh, that sort of thing…"

The following Monday, Tadashi submitted his first journal entry, entitled "A Terrible Saturday." With the grammar cleaned up, it went something like this:

On Saturday I had nothing to do. In the morning I sat in my room. In the afternoon, I decided to visit my grandmother. My grandmother lives far away. It usually takes 1.5 hours to go there, but on Saturday it took three hours…

[Here I expunge a detailed explanation of that extra hour and a half: a series of missed connections, train delays, road construction, etc.]

I walked from the local station to my grandmother's house. It takes 15 minutes to walk. It started to rain a little. When I got to my grandmother's house, I rang the doorbell, but she didn't answer. She wasn't home. All the doors were locked. I waited for half an hour. She didn't come back. I started walking back to the station. It began to rain very hard.
The end.

When I finally demanded an explanation for the new student's disconcerting glumness, my supervisor explained that Tadashi had been admitted to a community college in downtown Pittsburgh the previous fall, but had been mugged—on campus, in an elevator—within minutes of his arrival. He was sent back to Japan at once and had been undergoing therapy ever since.

Now, he was determined to try again, but his family was

concerned about his mental state. He already had the academic skills and test scores; the hope was that joining the class could restore his mojo. My job, then, is not so much to teach him as to prevent him from plunging from the fifth-floor windows of our classroom during breaks.

—◻—

The rest of our crew at the USIA Reading Room features the tall, sallow, Japanese-boy-band-cute Taro (journal themes: American movies, hot cars); stocky jock Kimiyasu (the NBA, Japanese and American professional baseball); and dwarfish wall-eyed Makoto (tedious daily routines of the sort that Tadashi tried to describe, only with less poignant outcomes). Rounding out the male roster is Tomohiro (his fiancée, Jesus), by far the oldest of the group at twenty-eight, with his horn-rimmed glasses and slicked back pompadour. He seeks admission to a California seminary.

The female contingent consists of the petite, perky Sachiko, eighteen years old going on twelve (Japanese boy bands, Taro); lanky, aggressively mannish, disgruntled Momoe (her growing dissatisfaction with our institute's teachers and classes); and the snowy-skinned and elegant Noriko (impressionistic painting, movies I could never sit through, cooking).

Earlier in my career I would have been disappointed to take charge of a class with so sparse a female enrollment. In those days, Noriko, twenty-two and just out of college, would have been the unwitting subject of fantasies far viler than such a fine young lady could ever imagine. But it's 1986 now and I'm recently married, and a Recently Married Man—caught in that awkward phase between Unmarried and Jadedly Married—denies himself any such indulgences as a "fantasy life" with a self-congratulatory pat on the back.

Indeed, these three girls are students under my charge. Somebody's daughters! What had I been thinking all those years? Henceforth, I have vowed, I shall be a respectable, upright member of the teaching profession, a vow that merits another pat on the back. Now, with both hands patting my own back, there is no danger that either will stray.

I'm not only merely married, I'm really most sincerely married.

—◻—

I've even been reading the Bible of late, which gives me something to discuss with Tomohiro when we exchange messages in his weekly journal notebook. Tomohiro is the group's most avid journalist, always exceeding the assigned minimum wordage by far.

He writes about his adoration for his fiancée in pure and dignified phrases that would not be out of place in a seventeenth-century Puritan's diary. He expresses his love of Jesus in similarly chaste terms. He explains and laments the difficulties of proselytizing in heathen Japan. All of which makes for good reading despite his rather dicey grasp of English grammar and mechanics.

Particularly jarring is his tendency to render the word *father* as *farter*, no small matter given the great esteem in which he holds his own dad, who is that rarest of birds in Japan, an evangelical Protestant preacher. *I have always looked to my farter for guidance*, he has confided.

The Christian community in greater Tokyo is a small one, so perhaps it's not all that surprising that his fiancée's father, too, is an ordained minister. He gets nervous whenever he encounters this unfamiliar new farter in his life, he admits.

One of the rules of journal writing is that the teacher will not correct errors. In contrast to the strictly marked academic assignments, journal writing is a chance for students to let their hair down and express themselves at length without any concern for grammatical accuracy. However, I have made an exception on more than one occasion with regard to this pivotal father/farter distinction. My markings tend to coax a few instances of correctly spelled *father*s from Tomohiro's pen, after which *farter*, like some resilient demon immune to exorcism, reclaims its turf.

Finally there came that fateful Saturday when Tomohiro's family visited his fiancée's family for dinner. The tension mounted through several paragraphs describing the arrangements for the feast, the selection of clothes, the seating arrangements…all building up to an even tenser passage describing the moment when the two distinguished Christian elders finally came face to face.

But not to worry: They got along famously. Indeed, this unforgettable evening then reached a climax when "we all knelt down so that my farter and her farter could lead us all in a prayer to the Holy Farter," at which point I flung the journal notebook as far as the walls of our cramped apartment would permit, sure it was possessed.

—◻︎—

But all that is neither here nor there. You must excuse me—I never begrudge myself any opportunity to tell the Holy Farter story. Who could? Let me bring us back now to the USIA Reading Room, where I've planted Tadashi in an interior corner far from the windows to act as a sort of reverse reading lamp, absorbing rather than giving light, while I help the others work with such resource-finding technologies as exist in the year 1986: mainly the handsomely varnished card catalogue and the pale green bound volumes of the *Reader's Guide to Periodical Literature*. I am using the latter to show the three girls how to search for magazine articles while Tomohiro eagerly cruises the stacks in search of sources for his research project on the history of missionary work in Tokyo.

My chores completed, I let the class run on autopilot; I circulate and facilitate where I can, narrowing a subject search here, diving into the magazine archives there…and so another splendid day amid a splendidly satisfying career in language education toots and whistles along its merry way when *Wham!,* out of nowhere comes the Found Object yet again in the form of Noriko's exquisite alabaster cleavage hovering just above the Fall 1985 volume of the *Reader's Guide* in all its glory.*

This development is quite literally stunning—it knocks me back two paces, one for each cleavical. This is a function of the astonishing beauty of Noriko's cleavage which, though by no means the stuff of a late-Sixties *Playboy* centerfold in terms of bulk, is classically contoured and just so utterly, fabulously *there*. I can't help thinking how my ninth-grade algebra teacher Mr. Conklin would have rejoiced at the sight of these twin parabolas with their perfectly balanced x and y axes.

Being the prim and proper young lady that she is, Noriko has up till now given the class's masturbating bloc precious little to work with. Today, however, she has worn a white boatneck blouse which showcases her fine collarbones and, as it turns out, a whole lot more when the wearer is poring (and pouring) over a volume of the *Reader's Guide to Periodic Literature* laid flat on a one-meter-high bookshelf.

I allow myself to take in this sight, accepting it as a rare and momentary gift that should not be squandered, like spotting Western lowland gorillas bounding through the mists. But no, the opportunity is not momentary. These gorillas aren't bounding. They are still. Check that: They *are* moving ever so subtly, ever so mesmerizingly—shifting, jostling…there's a word I am trying to avoid because it is just too creepy even for the likes of me…*jiggling!*…well, there it is—but the point is, the things aren't going anywhere. Never has a man felt so indebted to the editors of the *Reader's Guide to Periodical Literature* for their singularly exasperating and time-consuming system of subject categorization and cross-referencing as I do at this moment.

A thoroughly instinctive sleazeball, I immediately note that another meter-high bookshelf some dozen feet away from the one at which Noriko is stationed affords the optimal view, and that planting a random book on top of it provides me an excuse to be standing here should Noriko's anti-perv radar suddenly kick in. But

---

* By which I mean the cleavage's glory, not the *Reader's Guide*'s.

her anti-perv radar does *not* kick in and the view just goes on and on and on…until finally the ineluctable factoid of being Recently Married reasserts its grip and torpedoes the whole enterprise.

—□—

Deep down, a part of me is already looking forward to the Jadedly Married phase wherein a man can justify this type of sordid self-indulgence with bromides like "I read somewhere that this is good for my cardiovascular system"—but it's far too early for that now, and I know it. Recently Married *and* a professional teacher—a teacher in charge of Noriko's class—and yet treating her like an object, a toy! Ah, the shame of it all.

I finally, reluctantly skulk off to the side, out of temptation's range, in search of opportunities to facilitate learning, and then cast a glance over my shoulder just in time to see Kimiyasu wander toward my former perch and execute a perfect sitcom spit-take when he spies Noriko's parabolas. He soon discovers an unsuspected interest in Etruscan architecture (the topic of the random book that I have thoughtfully left out) and remains slack-jawed in the kill zone for a full minute before stalking stiffly away in the general direction of the restroom. [See Figure 3, following page.]

Makoto ambles by next, and is likewise ambushed. While I can't honestly say that I enjoy ogling the oglers as much as I enjoyed being a first-degree ogler myself, this new pastime does provide its own pleasures and, as a bonus, is virtually guilt-free. I have to suppress the urge to toss a coin or some such small, gleaming object into the No Man's Land between the two low bookshelves, thus provoking Noriko's line of sight to rise so that she can receive the full brunt of the jack-o-lantern grin on Makoto's face as he makes just-south-of-eye contact with her.

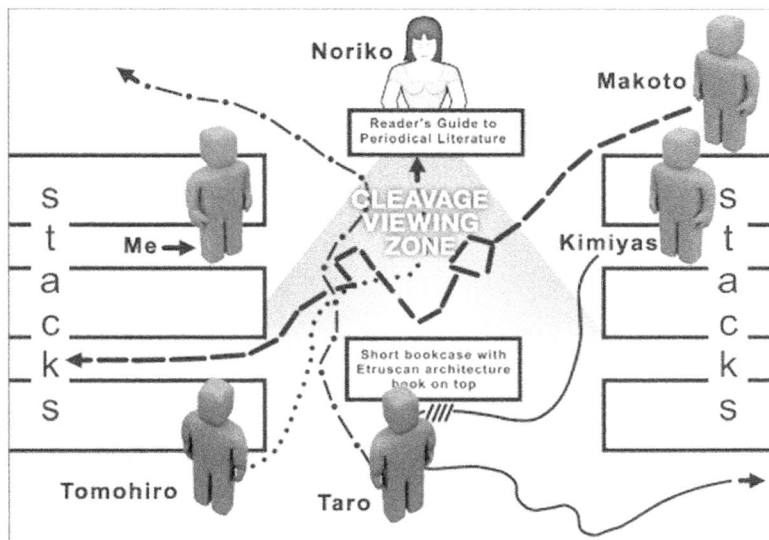

Figure 3: USIA Reading Room movements of male classmates vis-à-vis Noriko's prominent display of cleavage while bent over the Reader's Guide to Periodical Literature.

Makoto pirouettes dazedly away; Taro cards in for his shift; finally, Tomohiro steps up. Upon accessing the scene, he soon abandons Etruscan architecture and wades forth into No Man's Land. I assume he is about to clear his throat or in some way bring Noriko out of her source-searching reverie so as to preserve her dignity—unaware that that horse left the barn some time ago—but instead he stops five feet out, in the direct line of fire. And stares.

And stares.

And stares.

Three years hence, iconic film footage will emerge from China of a lone protester standing in the middle of a broad street, calmly facing down a row of tanks in the aftermath of protests in Tiananmen Square. That footage will remind me of how Tomohiro now boldly stands in the center of the kill zone, gazing serenely into Noriko's awesome guns.

It seems impossible that Noriko can be unaware of his presence. His legs, all three of them, now lie within the upper arc of her peripheral vision. And yet she continues running her index finger down row after row of cramped, blotchy text, oblivious. The show, it appears, really must go on. And I develop a suspicion that Tomohiro is going to skip the whole Recently Married phase of connubial bliss.

I find myself offended. At least, I think that's what I am. It's an unfamiliar emotion for me. The thing is, even perverts have an ethical code. It may not be written down anywhere—I could check the card catalogue, I suppose—but we all know it, and Tomohiro is blatantly ignoring that code, not to mention common sense. I amble by and clear my throat, which jerks him back into the temporal world.

"Finding everything you need?" I ask him.

"Yes, yes," he gasps. "I think so."

"Well, let me know if you need any help."

Sachiko approaches me with a question about encyclopedias. When I return to the scene of the crime, I expect to find it free of oglers. However, not only is Noriko still exhibiting her wares, but she is now doing so for yet another newly minted Etruscan architecture buff, one whom at first I cannot quite recognize owing to the smile that is now splitting his face for the first time in memory.

Let us all give thanks to Our Farter Who Farts in Heaven, Creator of the World and of all the beautiful and life-sustaining marvels in it. For in His wisdom, He appears to have cured Tadashi.

14. The Kitchen Murder Weapon Wussie Test

Suppose you found yourself in a life-and-death struggle with a burly prowler. With which of these kitchen implements would you be able to kill him? Check all that apply.

___ Carving knife (1 point)

___ Rolling pin (2 points)

___ Steak knife (3 points)

___ Bread knife (4 points)

___ Cutting board (5 points)

___ Fork (6 points)

___ Corkscrew (7 points)

___ Grapefruit spoon (8 points)

___ Butter knife (11 points)

___ Teaspoon (12 points)

___ Colander (13 points)

___ Microwave oven (14 points)

___ Spatula (17 points)

___ "World's Coolest Grandma" fridge magnet (24 points)

___ Turkey baster (27 points)

___ Oven mitt (30 points)

TOTAL: _____

Scoring: If you even read this page past the premise, you're no wussie.

15. *Great Wussies I Have Known, Vol. 2*
Wuss-Off at the Lobster Table

It was still a jot before noon as I piloted the Mortonville Missile into Northeast Harbor, where I stopped to get my bearings before heading out on Harborside Road. The Atlantic offered little flirtatious glimpses of itself here and there from behind the cool, dark drape of conifers to my right as I pondered what a perfect day it was to kick off Labor Day Weekend. Lost in this reverie, I nearly missed the gap in the high hedges I was looking for but managed to skid-turn up the winding private road.

I parked in a circular driveway of gray gravel in front of an enormous white house. The front door was propped open and I was tempted to walk right in but then thought better of it. So I stayed on the porch and knocked on the screen door…and knocked…and knocked with increasing vigor, supplementing the knuckle action with foppish *Yoo-hoo*s until I caught sight of a pallid creature inside, peeping around the corner from the living room.

"Yes?" said Pallid Creature as he trickled into view.

"Hi. I'm, uh, looking for Ruby?"

"Yes?"

"Or maybe Gail? Or Peg?"

"Or Peg. Oh, yes. Peg. Yes?"

His eyes were heavy-lidded and shifty, seemingly drawn to a lazily circling fly that I could not see. His fingers, craving employment, repeatedly slithered through his ash blond locks. He stopped three steps short of the screen door and gave the impression that nothing short of a volley of beebees fired at his feet from behind would impel him further in my direction.

As that appeared unlikely, I tapped on the door in an attempt to recapture his attention. Given our relative positions vis-à-vis the screen door mesh, this act almost literally constituted rattling his cage.

"Are the girls, uh, here?"

"The girls? Oh, I see—the girls! Oh…I'm afraid not."

He wore a white shirt with a starched collar of the type suggestive of sailing or some species of marine activity. It had two breast pockets large enough to contain some very hefty breasts, which he did not possess, making him seem perhaps more petite than he was. I guessed him to be about my own age or, if anything, younger. (I was twenty that Bicentennial summer.)

Later, while reviewing the mental video of this first encounter, I realized that we were at that moment two men with but a single thought, and that thought was: *Who is this odd, jittery interloper, and what is he doing at my house?*

"I'm Josh, by the way."

"I…I see."

"Who are you?"

This was evidently the wrong approach. He reacted as if I had snapped a wet gym towel at his groin—an expression I recognized instinctively.

"I'm *Mmmawnnn*," he said by way of introduction, the wayward fingers having now migrated from his hair to his mouth, muffling his speech.

It was becoming increasingly clear that no invitation to come in and wait for the return of the girls would be forthcoming.

"Well, then. I guess I'll go into town for lunch. If I dropped back around two, do you suppose the girls would be here?"

"Yes! Yes! Oh, yes, that would be much better!"

"All righty, then."

"Oh, yes. Yes, the girls…"

And although I could not see him, I was somehow certain that he remained rooted to the spot all the while as I returned to my '70 Dodge Challenger and rounded the gravel loop that returned me to the long paved access road, and kept watching me until the high hedge that bounded the immense yard swallowed me up.

—¤—

Shortly after two that afternoon Ruby emerged through the same screen door and onto the porch, where Pallid Creatures fear to tread. There was a song on Bruce Springsteen's most recent album—something about some girl dancing across some porch like something or other while some radio song played—that came to mind at that moment. The song's narrator had arrived in a hot car in the hopes of taking said porch-dancing personage away with him, fittingly enough.

You ain't a beauty, but hey, you're all right—so went the only recollectable lyric, but I couldn't sing that to Ruby because, well, I was self-conscious about singing on porches in broad daylight and more to the point, over the course of the ten days I had spent with her back in June, she truly had evolved into a beauty in my eyes: Those too-perfect cheekbones, the long Modigliani face split by the bowed lips, the beanpole frame swathed in the signature pastel-blue peasant blouse with the puffy short sleeves—she had not changed a jot since our parting at the front end of the Summer of Seventy-six.

Throughout my long self-imposed exile in the Green Mountains of Vermont I had thought of nothing but Ruby's face. Okay, that's a lie: I had thought about handjobs, too. And about Ronald Reagan. But not in the same context.

But I digress. Kindly indulge a switch into flashback mode via some pretentious italics to catch the reader up.

—¤—

In June of my twenty-first year, I spent ten days slowly driving from Minnesota to New England with three pretty college girls in a sleek forest-green muscle car.

If there were ever a more auspicious opening line than that for a letter to Penthouse Forum, I have yet to see it. Alas, the account following that lede would bitterly disappoint the loyal readers of that venerable publication—unless, of course, I were to thumb my nose at the Forum contributors' Code of Honor and just make stuff up.

It all began in April, actually, when I had attended a party at the home of Ruby—fellow part-timer at a printing company, former housemate of a girl I had briefly dated, and all-around extra in the cinematic saga that was my undergraduate life—during which she approached me with the following scheme, enunciated in that urgent, curlicue intonation that is so irksome coming from many young ladies and yet so oddly enchanting coming from Ruby:

"Josh? Is it true that you're going to New England? For a summer job? Oh, really? Vermont! Well, Gail and I and this one other girl? Peg? We're going to Maine! Isn't that neat? Right next door to you! We're going to be, like, housekeepers? For this really rich family? They've got a huge summer home right on the ocean? Yeah, so..."

As was her wont, she laid three fingers lightly across my forearm in the midst of this spiel, as if needing assurance that I kept a pulse. Her touch felt oddly cool, the tactile equivalent of a strong mint. At such moments I had to remind myself that she was the long-time companion of Harry the Moss-Eater, who was very much still in the picture. And not just the metaphorical picture, but within my actual field of vision, passing a bong around with some Moss-Eater brethren over in the corner. Meanwhile, Ruby kept rattling off inquiries:

"By the way, when does your job start? Uh-huh. And how were you planning to get there? Oh, you're driving out? Really? Well, see, me and Gail and Peg—that's the other girl? Did I mention her?—Do you know Peg?—anyway, we were wondering if you'd be okay with maybe going together? Like, taking us out there in...in your car? Us three girls?"

And how did she think Harry might react if he learned of this scheme, I asked in a conspiratorial whisper; and she assured me that he was already in the loop and felt just ducky about it. I followed up by inquiring as to whether the other two girls had boyfriends and if so, whether they, too, would prove to be so open-minded, and her reply revealed that the whole plan had long since been *aired to the wider Mankato State community. Had I not gone to the party, I might have read about it in the* Free Press *the next day under the headline "Local Wussie Enlisted as Cross-Country Driver."*

"Gail's boyfriend—Do you remember Gail? Well, her boyfriend, he really didn't like the idea at first? Of Gail going all that way in a guy's car? But then we, like, told him that the guy would be you? And then he was, like, okay? Because, he said, like, everybody knows you're harmless, Josh."

I was stunned. Cut to the quick. Taken aback, even. I began to protest that I was not harmless, not remotely so, but having no proof to back up my claim, finally had no choice but to swallow this calumny—for the time being.

That, then, is why I ended up surrendering my car to three virtual strangers: to bide my time for a chance to prove myself harmlessness-less. It would take a quarter century of reflection for me to realize how easily I had been duped. It wasn't merely that girls were always thinking four chess moves ahead of me; it was that I was playing checkers.

—◻—

And so we embarked one sunny June morning with a U-Haul trailer attached to the back of the Missile. Over the next week Ruby and Gail would navigate a capricious route from Mankato through Duluth, across Michigan's Upper Peninsula, over a wide swath of Ontario, lengthwise across New York State, then up the rugged Maine coast to the stately summer home of the Minton family.

We stopped frequently at Ruby and Gail's whim to climb allegedly pretty rock formations, peer into Niagara Falls, bathe in the light of the Canadian moon, sightsee in Boston, and, of course, buy more beer and wine. Except for one night in a motel room, we slept in a tent. On the even-numbered nights, I got handjobs.

It was Peg who doled out these kindnesses. She was a sturdy, dark-complected girl with big, soulful eyes and boyishly short brown hair and firm, perfectly spherical bosoms that I was allowed to manipulate during the procedures. My offer to reciprocate her manual favors was accepted only once, at the end of the trip, so I was mystified as to the motive for her largesse, being as we had just met.

Years later, having had my numerous faults catalogued for me the way only a spouse of many years can do it, I would look back and arrive at the realization that the girls must have convened a secret powwow along about Day Two on the subject of my grumpiness.

"Josh is harshing our mellow," someone—I'm betting Gail—had said. It seemed that no matter how much marijuana smoke, wine and beer was pumped into me in the course of a day's journey, and it was a lot, I just couldn't relax—kept squirming in my seat like an eight-year-old bound for Sunday School, barely spoke except to make some sarcastic wisecrack, etc.

On top of which, there was the awkward move I had put on Gail the first night in the tent. The blond and perky Gail was objectively the most attractive of the three, besides which she was lying right next to me at the time, and I was still smarting from her boyfriend's insensitive gibe. "Harmless, huh? Well, who's harmless now, eh, buddy?" I whispered as I reached for what I thought to be Gail's shoulder but was in fact her calf and got kicked hard in the face.

Clearly, the girls agreed, this sort of behavior could not be tolerated, and someone would have to sacrifice herself for the good of the group. The consensus quickly fell on the boyfriendless Peg.

She had thick, marbled arms so that one never need fear her pooping out halfway through her self-assigned task. She was expert at varying torque and speed, and ambidextrous to boot. Despite these noble qualities of Peg's, at the time I would try to imagine Ruby's slender, minty fingers performing the act and visualize her face, while simultaneously keeping Peg's entirely satisfactory bosoms in the picture.

That's an awful lot of mental juxtaposing to pull off, especially after a long day of driving, drinking, toking, and overhearing nonstop female discourse. But I toughed it out, and I suppose Peg's ministrations had the desired effect, for I now cherish the memories of that whole trip, handjobless days included.

—◻—

Our last two nights together were spent in the Minton mansion outside Northeast Harbor, Maine. The family, it turned out, had been delayed a week and I had a few days free before I had to report for duty as dishwasher at a snooty tennis lodge in Vermont.

I claimed the master bedroom so that I could boast of having slept in a multimillionaire's bed. We smoked still more weed and went to Geddy's Pub that first night. In the morning I performed W.C. Handy blues tunes on the grand piano in the spacious, sunny parlor while Ruby sprawled across it like a chanteuse and eyed me adoringly.

Then we lounged in matching rocking chairs and sunned ourselves on the deck as the Atlantic massaged the slatey boulders below us. The boulders, I thought, looked fake, rather like the boulders that an actor in a lizard costume would brandish over his head in a lesser Star Trek *episode. But that was probably just the weed.*

"What are we gonna do today, Josh?" Ruby asked.

"Oh, let us go into town," I said, pursing my lips and over-articulating my consonants in my best guess at how Eastern Old Money talked. "We could throw money on the street and watch the peasants grovel for it. They grovel so well this time of year." And Ruby giggled a long, happy, stoned giggle at that. And then I had to leave.

In August I got a letter from her asking if I was still there? And would I be able to drive out? For Labor Day weekend? Before everyone headed back to Minnesota?

All of which was prelude to my initial encounter with Pallid Creature.

—¤—

As I was saying, then, Ruby came out to the porch to greet me on my return to the Minton house. This I found immediately curious. Why didn't she let me in? Why couldn't I play my piano again? And sit in my rocker, and lie in my bed?

"Oh, Josh?" Ruby said, "Did you get here around noon? Did you talk to Edward?" [Onset of hug] "Oh, *Josh!* How was the drive?" [Termination of hug] "Edward's very upset, you know?"

"Who," I asked, "is Edward?"

"Edward? Didn't you meet Edward? Edward," she said, dropping into a whisper, "is Mrs. Minton's son from her first marriage. Didn't you meet Edward, Josh?"

I pulled myself out of a post-hug daze and acknowledged to Ruby a faint memory of meeting Edward—for I assumed by process of elimination that the Pallid Creature who had been so niggardly of his self-introduction was the very man—but pleaded ignorance as to how I might have been the cause of his wounded mental state.

"But is it your fault, Josh? I don't think so. No, no, no. Never mind," assured Ruby. Then she led me down the porch steps toward my car.

"I have a few things to tell you? I'm afraid Peg—remember Peg? She left this morning."

"Oh, really?"

"Gail went back last weekend..."

"Ah."

She stroked my arm again, which somehow made me anticipate still more bad news.

"The thing is, Josh? You can't stay in the house."

"What?"

"I'm afraid that Edward— You know Edward? Edward would be really upset if you even came in."

"Huh? Where do I stay, then?"

"You remember Harry? Harry's here. He brought a tent? There's a field down the road a few miles? So you'll be camping with Harry, won't you?"

—◻—

At Geddy's that night Harry said, "This Edward character kind of gums everything up. He was supposed to leave with the family last week, but, well, he didn't. So now we have to work around him."

"But can't he understand," I pleaded, "that that's *my house?*"

"Yeah, I heard you made yourself right at home last time," Harry bellowed. He was the sort of fellow that is often described as "A great big bear of a man—warm, affable, always with the ready smile and the slap on the back" by the sort of writer given to bear-vs.-large-hairy-man analogies, though his thick black mustache suggested more the walrus for my money. He wore flannel shirts over a bulky, well-padded frame that made for something of a sight gag when paired with Ruby's almost anorexic petiteness. He was in his mid-twenties and a year from finishing a business degree.

"For what it's worth," Harry said, "I made the same mistake you did."

"What mistake is that?"

"Driving right up to the house and knocking on the front door. It freaked poor old Edward out."

"It did?"

"And that's why he freaked even more when *you* did it later on."

"He did?"

"Poor bastard's probably sitting up there right now wondering how many more of these Minnesota bozos are gonna show up." We all giggled at this, still feeling the effects of Harry's Thai stick from the drive over.

"What's up with this Edward?" I asked. "Is he in college?"

"College? Oh, he's not in college, is he? His mother told me he just turned…thirty?"

"*Thirty!* What does he do?"

"Do? You mean, like a job? He doesn't *do* anything, does he?"

"How long has he been there? All summer?"

"Yes, all summer. Hasn't he? He came with his mother… Didn't he?"

"So, why is he still there?"

"I don't really know."

"What does he do with himself all day?"

"You mean, like, hobbies? He has a sailboat? He went out on it a few times?"

"To fish?"

"No, he doesn't fish, does he? Just to, you know…sail?"

"And that's it?"

"Pretty much. He shows up for, like, meals?"

"Did he flirt with you guys?"

"Edward? Oh, no, no. Edward wouldn't do that, would he?"

"What on earth is wrong with him?"

A single rich guy at thirty, to my thinking, ought to be a playboy. He ought to amble around in ascots and a pencil-thin mustache and slicked-back hair, and have a confident, huffing sort of laugh, and say "What ho!" at least once a day and cheerfully grab the cute hired help by the butt-cheeks at least twice a week—even if he happens to be gay.

I felt strongly about these things. This Edward character sucked at being rich.

—◻—

My memories of the rest of Labor Day weekend 1976 are a bit smudgy. After acquiring a twelve-pack and dropping off Ruby, Harry led me to the campsite he had found, an open expanse curtained off by pines on an undeveloped hillock belonging to some Astor or Pierrpont.

We resolved to make the best of our unexpectedly rustic accommodations, and so, under a too-bright-for-comfort full moon we worked our way through the beer and another clump of Thai stick while listening to an unaccountably hilarious episode of Radio Mystery Theater on the car radio, after which we set up the tent.

Later this proved to be a regrettable sequencing of events because we unwittingly pitched the tent on a slope. In the course of the night, Newtonian physics inexorably pulled Harry downhill like some sort of mustachioed mudslide, nearly smothering me. That led to an awkward moment in the morning, which we papered over with a thoroughly heterosexual breakfast of beer and Thai stick and peanut M&Ms, which neatly set the pace for the whole day.

"It's a holiday," we told each other, for it is customary among

Minnesotans to establish some sort of rationale before embarking on a long day of ceaseless substance abuse.*

I was delighted to let Harry handle all the drunk-driving duties, as nothing seemed to impair him. He never let us down. Along the coast of Maine that Labor Day weekend of '76, we would pass many a scene of troopers arresting badly weaving bluebloods, one of whom would later become President of the United States of America. Harry's judgment as to when to slow down and when to speed up easily surpassed that fellow's. Harry was the true Decider.

Back in Mankato Harry and I had not been chummy. My friends and I had forged an uneasy alliance with Harry's clique, whom my friend Durward had snidely dubbed "the Moss-Eaters" owing to what we felt was their excessive affinity for the great outdoors and simple living. A couple of them resided in a shack outside of town with a bona fide outhouse, and the whole bunch would spend vacations together engaged in such eccentric diversions as hiking the Appalachian Trail. Their womenfolk wore overalls and some left their armpits unshaved, but they seemed to have more fun than we did. Ergo, we eyed them with suspicion.

Harry, a Moss-Eater elder, was the first of the tribe I would come to know, and over that lost weekend we bonded. I was glad that I had been too cowardly to put the patented Muggins Moves on his girlfriend when such opportunities had arisen back in June, for it would have made our time together now even more awkward than it already was—starting the day off, as we had, in a mildewy embrace. Harmlessness has its virtues, I suppose.

—◻—

On the eve of the last day of the long weekend, Ruby conveyed to Harry and me Edward's invitation to join him for lunch. We didn't know what to make of that and decided that a little more Thai stick might help us figure it out, but instead we got off on a tangent

---

* A Minnesotan knows that he really does have a substance abuse problem when the rationales devolve to the likes of "It's a day."

about how awesome the Jerry Lewis Telethon used to be back when they had that actor who wore a dark leotard and sat on a stool on a bare stage and did the ominous "I Am Muscular Dystrophy" monologue. Then we drank more beer. At least, we were pretty sure he sat on a stool.

We bought live lobsters right off the docks the next day (meaning that Harry did, actually, while I watched) and brought them to the house, where Ruby was finally authorized to let us inside through the kitchen. We were early: Edward would not be ready to receive us until one or so, and so we killed time with lobster races across the kitchen floor. I named mine Spot and bonded with him (I was bonding right and left that weekend), and then dropped him into a pot of seething water, causing him to scream. It was a reaction I hadn't expected and it was, I felt strongly, very uncool of Spot.

Sensing my distress, Harry led me out of the kitchen to a damp outdoor storage area for our appetizer, one last soothing bowl of Thai stick.

"But, *why* does Edward suddenly want to have lunch with us?" I asked.

"Hell if I know. I suppose maybe he wants to face his demons or something."

"So we're the demons?"

"Guess so." He took a big hit and wheezed, then added, "I dunno. He struck me as a pretty lonely guy. Maybe he just wants to be friendly."

"Oh, yeah, friendly," I groused. "Won't let us come in the house all weekend, but *now* he wants to be friends? Bet he doesn't even have any friends." Truth be told, I was still upset about the nasty demise of Spot.

At this point Ruby appeared and began frantically jabbing her finger upward. We found the gesture unbearably hilarious until we figured out that it was universal sign language for "Edward's sitting on the deck right above you and can hear, maybe even smell you." Back in the kitchen Ruby scolded us in her regular language. "Is

Edward such a bad guy? Did he ever do anything to you? I know you don't like him, but he's not such a bad guy. Is he?"

I got a sinking feeling in my stomach, a certain premonition…

"I mean, basically isn't he…"

No! No! Don't say it, Ruby!

"…isn't he harmless?"

At that moment, I resolved to be forever Edward's enemy. First he had appropriated my house and now he had appropriated my adjective. Plus, he'd made Ruby cross with me.

—◻—

In the dining room, we found Edward at the end of a long table, once again twirling his hair and jerkily following the flight of that invisible fly. Ruby seated me at the opposite end. Harry sat in the middle and, when she had finished laying out the spread, Ruby took the chair across from him. Eyeing Edward, I wondered momentarily which of us was the daddy in this arrangement.

"Have you…have you ever had lobster before?" asked Edward.

He flinched, perhaps thinking that we would take offense at the question. Harry said that he had tried some in a restaurant up to the Cities one time, but it had been de-shelled. I confessed to being a lobster virgin. I knew it would become apparent as soon as the deconstruction of Spot, now glowering redly at me from the plate below, got underway.

Having risked controversy once with his daring probe re the breadth of our lobster experience, Edward retreated into his shell while I labored mightily to extract Spot from his. Impaired as I was, I had a hard time gauging how much force to apply to the shell cracker and thus intermittently sent chunks of Spot-shrapnel spiraling off toward my fellow diners at alarming velocity.

"So, Edward," I heard myself say over the cacophony of cracks, "I hear your family is friendly with Vice President Rockefeller and his wife."

"Um, yes, well… Umm, the Rockefellers… Yes, mother is an old friend of Happy's."

"Must have been tense times for everyone last year. I mean, what with President Ford getting shot at right and left—*hee-hee!*"

It wasn't the prospect of presidential assassination that caused me to giggle, but rather the end-over-end trajectory of a trapezoid-shaped shard of claw that rocketed higher than my head.

"Oh, yes, right. Well, I suppose so. A nasty thing, isn't it, getting shot at? Not that I would know personally. Have you…have you ever been shot at?"

"Me? No…no, not as I recall. Ruby, have you ever been shot at?"

"No, Josh."

"Harry?"

"Uh, nope."

"Ah. Well, then," said Edward.

"Ah," I concurred.

"Do you…follow politics, then?" asked Edward.

"I try to keep up."

Harry was busy sucking the meat from remote precincts of his lobster much the same way that he sucked the marrow out of life, while Ruby swung her attention from Edward to me and back again as if watching Bjorn Borg and Ilie Nastase in the Wimbledon final. An uncommonly tepid sexual tension filled the air as Edward and I competed for the title of Ruby's Second Favorite Man at the Table.

"It's interesting…isn't it?" Edward cautiously volunteered. "Politics, I mean."

"Do you think so?" I said, knowing that it would rattle him.

"Well, that is to say… I mean, it's an election year… Isn't it?"

"Well, yes, but it's not as interesting as people make it out to be," I heard myself prattle as I downshifted into political-geek mode. "I mean, people made a big deal out of Ronald Reagan all summer, but there was never any way that Reagan was going to get the Republican nomination."

"Oh, no?"

"Oh, God no. Not that numbnut— Er, that fellow. The man's *wa-a-ay* too conservative ever to win a general election, you know."

"I see."

"Of course, I'm all for Carter but—"

"Oh, really? Why is that?"

Damn, he's fighting back, my subconscious mind registered, before adding, *The last time I got a handjob, it was in a room directly over our heads.* I banished that intrusive thought and refocused on Edward's unexpectedly aggressive interruption.

"Well, he's a breath of fresh air, isn't he? Someone from outside Washington, someone with no connection to Richard Nixon, right? After what we've been through, eight years of Jimmy Carter would be like…like the first spring breeze after a long winter."

"That's beautiful, Josh. Isn't that beautiful, Harry? But Josh, stop eating that part. It's the part that has Spot's poop in it, isn't it?"

"Oh."

"So," Edward said, "you'll be voting Democratic, then?"

"Oh, yes. But it won't do any good."

"It won't?"

"No, no. I don't put any stock in these polls. Mark my words, Ford will win the election."

"Ah. Ah, yes. I see," he said, smartly halving a claw with the daintiest of cracks.

"Um-hmm."

"I…I suppose Carter is just a flash in the pan, then…if that's the correct expression?"

I pontificated at length on the theme of Jimmy Carter's bright political future—how he and his good buddy Edward Kennedy would team up to win the following two elections and together make the Eighties a veritable Golden Age of progressive social and economic policy.

"Fascinating," Edward said. "Yes, yes. Oh, I see. Yes. I'm sure you're right."

Ruby gave me that adoring look again, the one she had granted me that time I had played the grand piano, for I had categorically overawed my foe with the sheer gravitas of my vast, infallible political erudition. I had won the Lobster Table Wuss-off, and had revealed myself to be something incrementally shy of totally harmless.

—◻—

I even came to feel sorry for Edward, as he sullenly finished his meal and excused himself. For unlike him, I had friends. I might not be the most spontaneous, outgoing guy on the block myself, but at least I had friends who took me out to places like Niagara Falls and Geddy's Pub, or down to the docks to buy fresh lobsters, friends who arranged the occasional gratuitous handjob for me; while Edward was fated forever to be alone and afraid, unloved and unrubbed. Even on his own deck he would ever after sit in fear of overhearing his demons taking stoned, snarky potshots at him from Somewhere Down Below.

An hour later in the circular driveway, I hugged Ruby with what for me passes for real feeling, then shook hands with Harry (a pump-primer) and Edward (a dead fish). The couple would head back to Mankato the following day while I would remain in Vermont until winter.

Who knew when we might meet again? It was a chilling moment, or would have been if not for the effete corps of impudent snobs that drove up in a gigantic boat of a convertible at that moment, one of them shouting, "Eddie! *Whaddaya say there, Eddie-boy!* Hop in, will ya? We're off to see the sailboat races!"

16. Pornography: The Wussie's Default BFF

The idea of a baseball game on a sunny spring or summer day was the spontaneity of going. "Let's go the park!" you'd say at 2 o'clock when the game was to be played at 3 o'clock in the afternoon. "Let's go to the bleachers!" And you'd go and you'd get a ticket and you'd sit down... And it was the spontaneity of it! And sitting there in the sunshine and watching experts— good, skilled craftsmen—ply their trade.

– Studs Terkel in the PBS *Baseball* documentary

I often recall those words and the radiant glee with which the sprightly, twinkly, oddly leprechaun-like Studs warbled them, for they capture so well the way that a great many wussies feel about good old American smut.

Not that we would sit out in the bleachers in the afternoon sunshine to enjoy our pornography. I'd edit that part out of my personal paean to porn. And the more inclusive crafts*people* ought to be applied. But otherwise, we smut-loving wussies and Studs are very much on the same page.

Studs expresses his appreciation for the sound fundamentals practiced by the practitioners of his beloved game. We wussies similarly cherish the subtleties of properly constructed porn. Studs likes the smoothly-executed double play; so, in our own way, do many of us. He can enthuse about the fluidity with which a batter turns his hips as he lays into a ball; we can thrill to the fluidity with which an actress turns her hips to lay into some balls. I could go on like this for a full page, but I fear the reader tires.

The take-home point is simply that, like Studs, wussies can manage with little effort to persuade ourselves at times that the performers sweating away in front of us would gladly do what they do for the sheer joy of it, even without pay. And in both cases people will come. Oh yes, Ray, people will most definitely come.[*]

—◻—

Wussies like pornography not so much because we fear sex itself, but because we fear its consequences. For wussies, sexual encounters fall into two categories, each with its own terrifying perils: sex-for-money encounters ($\rightarrow$ diseases, rip-offs, the prospect of bumping into that eyebrowless freak played by Charlize Theron in her Oscar turn) and sex-for-soul encounters, aka marriage ($\rightarrow$ loss of free will, a humiliating public ceremony, children).

Pornography offers a window into a world that is positively Disneyesque in its ideality, a world where men seem to fear neither set of penalties while enjoying access to a far wider range of open-minded companions than any of us could ever hope to encounter in person.

It's not just the thrill of the naked and undulating horizontal lady—the purple mountains majesty above the fruited plain, as it were—that keeps bringing us back, then; it's also the breathtaking impetuousness—the *spontaneity* of it, as Studs put it. *Hey! Can that guy just up and do that?* we marvel. *Without getting HIV? Or ending up in a powder-blue tuxedo and frilly shirt, spewing out embarrassing poetry with a straight face in front of his college buddies? My god... Can he just* do *that?*

And then one rewinds a bit, just to be sure that...why, yes, evidently he just can.

---

[*] Sorry. That's all I got—I swear.

—◻—

Two qualifications here, lest the reader think even less of me than I deserve to be thought of.

First, the pornography I'm talking about is pretty tame stuff by contemporary standards. Here's a short list of subgenres I *don't* patronize:

anal
double penetration
mature (GILF)
she-males
BDSM
ass-to-mouth
fetish
gangbang
bukkake
wienie roast
peeing

All right, "wienie roast" isn't a real subgenre. But if it were, I'd stay the hell away from it.

No, call me an old-fashioned fuddy-duddy. Call me a hick from Squaresville. Call me a carbolated wallaby, for that matter, and see if I care. Wussie though I am, I know names will never hurt me. But I know what I like in porn, too, and the traditional forms of intercourse (oral, genital, digital), executed sequentially by one male and one female performer—okay, maybe two female performers— were good enough for grandpa and they're good enough for me.*

The other point I wish to make is that I support *American* pornography. In this day and age, when my motherland has long

---

* My maternal grandpa, that is. Can't say what the other one was into but in old family photos he strikes me as sort of a freak.

since surrendered all claims of supremacy in the manufacture of automobiles, computers, televisions, robots, blowjob simulators, and pretty much every other device whose primary function is not murder or mayhem, she can still boast the finest adult film industry in the world. Take that, Japan.

Please don't take me for a racist or protectionist here, either. I don't mind multiracial or international casts in my American pornography: indeed, I often insist on these things. Spending most of my time in Japan as I do, the participation in a scene of a Japanese woman or two never fails to give that scene a more down-home, wholesome vibe.

What I simply can't abide is the sight of Japanese women in *Japanese* pornography, given what so often befalls them. Now, I'll grant you that it's a wee bit late for me to launch a campaign for induction into the Feminist Writers Hall of Fame at this point in my career, but I cling to one heartfelt core belief that I hope all readers can get behind: If a man is doing something to a woman that is obviously causing her pain, and that man is not a medical professional doing something essential to said woman's well-being, then *the man should stop doing that thing immediately.*

Japanese pornographers evidently do not subscribe to this tenet,* and that's why I've soured on them. That, and all the peeing.

No, give me the good old red-white-and-deeply-blue American porn. Give me enthusiastic, take-charge females and docile, pliant, relatable males. Let me believe in a world where an earnest wussie like me can be minding his own business at home, hear the doorbell, be confronted by a scantily clad UPS delivery lady, and

---

* Indeed, Japanese pornographers generally insist that male performers maintain control and dominance over females at all times. This has one curious side effect: The overwhelming bulk of oral sex scenes in Japan show the male participant servicing the female one—at great length and with unflagging enthusiasm. *Don't think you can squirm away from me, missy,* the actors seem to be muttering into the nether regions of their female costars, who moan out unconvincing protests.

The lesson, as always: Never try to outwit a Japanese female.

soon find himself pinned to his own sofa, receiving her relentless ministrations to an equally relentless synthesized beat.

Let me believe in that splendiferous parallel universe where half-naked coeds go out of their way to stay after class to coax some vigorous private tutoring out of their flustered French teachers; where dedicated nurses go the extra mile to soothe a distraught patient; where good skilled craftspeople ply their trade, and where all good wussies go when they die.

17. *Profiles in Wussitude, Vol. 4*

Yammerin' Hank

Whatever may befall me, I trust that I may never lose my respect for purity in others. The subject of sex is one on which I do not wish to meet a man at all, unless I can meet him on the most inspiring grounds. I would preserve purity in act and thought as I would cherish the memory of my mother.

By the time David Henry Thoreau was thirty-six, the townsfolk of Concord, Massachusetts, from where he never strayed very far or for very long, had watched him cycle through the identities of teacher, surveyor, and writer; and these fellow citizens—the people who knew him best—had come to regard him as...well, a wholly passable surveyor. In fact, some would have called him a damned fine surveyor. Not a hall of famer, mind you, but solid. "If you want some surveyin' done," folks would have told you, "you could do worse than that fuzzy-necked feller over yonder, Thoreau. For anything else, best leave him be."

"And for God's sake, don't leave him alone out in the woods," another might then have interjected, with a shudder, for no one could forget that the sole mark on the local ecosystem made by this odd young man had been a carelessly set cooking fire some years earlier that had laid waste to three hundred acres of woodland.

It was at this very age of thirty-six that Thoreau devised, entirely on his own, a solution to a persisting problem. The laces of his boots were forever coming undone, much to the annoyance of anyone unfortunate enough to be dragged along with him on a long walk through the woods.

After experimenting with various materials for shoestrings, he one day decided to reverse the order of the laces while tying, thus producing a squarer-looking and much more stable binding than the granny knot that he had been using for decades. His friends tried to explain to him that his brainstorm, the "square knot," had in fact been around for eons, but to no avail.

— ¤ —

To the present-day wussie community, Thoreau is an icon not easily embraced. What Justice Clarence Thomas is to African Americans, what the late Malcolm Forbes is to gay Republicans, and what the actor Keanu Reeves is to cigar-store Indians, that is what Henry David Thoreau is to wussies: a pioneer who achieved great things while snubbing his own kind. Thoreau was a wussie through and through, but he was a self-loathing wussie. I mean, even more so than the rest of us.

But a wussie he most surely was. The most widely known facts of Thoreau's life qualify him as perhaps the most obvious choice for a Profile in Wussitude. There's all that raving of his about "purity" quoted above, just for starters. The strongest intoxicant he enjoyed was fresh air. He freeloaded off parents or friends for all his forty-four years of life—save the "two years, two months and two days" that he famously spent in a cabin of his own construction on Walden Pond. But even there he was squatting on Ralph Waldo Emerson's land, and, since he was little more than a mile from town, still managed to stroll home regularly to raid the fridge. Thoreau is so luminous, so flamboyant a wussie that beside him, even the likes of Hirohito and Thomas Jefferson and I can pass ourselves off as horny longshoremen spoiling for a brawl.

In this chapter, I seek to deconstruct this most complicated of wussies by examining by turns his five salient aspects: Thoreau the Adventurer, Thoreau the Radical, Thoreau the Cooze Hound, Thoreau the Writer, and Thoreau the Moss-Eater.

1. Thoreau the Adventurer

Thoreau yearned to be thought of as a traveler, an adventurer, a risk-taker. Eschewing the usual methods for earning these labels— i.e. traveling, having adventures, and taking risks—he took the novel approach of instead fuzzying up the definitions of the terms themselves to the point where they dovetailed with stuff he had already done.

For example, here's Thoreau on the subject of courage:

Bravery deals not so much in resolute action, as in healthy and assured rest. Its palmy state is staying at home... One moment of serene and confident life is more glorious than a whole campaign of daring.

If I'm reading him right, he's saying that for him, a good nap on the sofa trumps an Ecstasy-fueled road trip to Tijuana. Now, that in itself takes nerve—with bonus points for passing off *palmy* as a real word. "Every man is a warrior when he aspires," he concludes. Hmm. I've dared to dream of seeing some of my undergraduate students naked. I guess that makes me Rambo.

Here's Thoreau on travel:

In the spaces of thought are the reaches of land and water over which men go and come. The landscape lies fair within... [T]he biography of a man who has spent his days in a library, may be as interesting as the Peninsular campaign... For I measure distance inward and not outward. Within the compass of a man's ribs there is space and scene enough for any biography.

Translation: Either he's clairvoyantly anticipating that 1966 science fiction film in which Raquel Welch and Stephen Boyd shrink down and putter through a guy's bloodstream in a microscopic submarine, or he's saying that *reading* about faraway places is every bit as exhilarating and death-defying as actually *going* to them. And saying it in a deucedly convincing manner at that! Now *that*, my friends, is wussie genius in action.

Going by his own definition of travel, Thoreau spent his short life zestfully roaming the earth from South America to Greenland, from New Zealand to Germany. Meanwhile, his actual trips were so limited that, were they sexual encounters, he could barely be said to have achieved penetration. He made gingerly little pokes into nearby Maine and Quebec, as short and tentative and harmless as Karl Rove diddling a plus-sized DC streetwalker.

He did make one considerably longer trip: all the way to exotic Minnesota, in fact. But there he journeyed late in life while battling tuberculosis and only reluctantly, at the urging of his physician, a swarthy, dwarfish mulatto who advised him to strip naked and purify himself in the waters of Lake Minnetonka.

—¤—

Okay, I'm interpolating a little about the doctor, though the basis for the trip to Minnesota is true. But back to the question at hand: Can it truly be said that Thoreau was an adventurous traveler? Well, not if you listen to that big Scottish meanie Robert Louis

Stevenson, who managed to cram the words "womanish," "unmanly," "dastardly," and "fear" into one sentence on Thoreau. And that was just a prelude to this:

In one word, Thoreau was a skulker. He did not wish virtue to go out of him among his fellow-men, but slunk into a corner to hoard it for himself. He left all for the sake of certain virtuous self-indulgences.

So, there's that.

When it comes to actual acts of courage, though, Thoreau's trophy case is not entirely bare. In these three areas he certainly stacks up favorably vis-à-vis your more conventional wussies.

(1) As a writer, he bounced back from rejections and dealt aggressively with critics. This stands in stark contrast to the position I take in the face of poor reviews, namely fetal.

(2) Likewise, I duck and cover whenever an argument breaks out, but Thoreau was fervently disputatious and could turn any petty divergence of views into a brouhaha. "He wanted a fallacy to expose, a blunder to pillory," sighed Emerson, who liked to yank his young disciple's chain from time to time by tossing out verbal hand grenades in his presence along the lines of "I believe Rhode Island to be bigger than Texas," just for the fun of watching Thoreau go off, and Thoreau never seemed to wise up to the game. One is left wondering whether Thoreau reversed the order of his given names to Henry David just to let his parents know that they had gotten it wrong.

(3) Most notably, he nursed his brother through the final days of a lethal tetanus infection. I don't really have a joke here. I for one could not have done that.

To sum up, Thoreau was fearless in disputes that had a zero chance of escalating into knifeplay and unflinching in interaction with patients suffering from horrible but noncontagious diseases.

—◻—

If you define courage as the ability to do things that you're scared to do, then we wussies have the easiest row to hoe, given that we fear doing just about anything. However, most people would agree that a demonstration of true courage requires a conscious decision to face down some real, palpable danger—that it entails a risk of painful consequences, typically through involvement in some sort of battle or struggle or Sarah Palin interview or some such.

But there was only one known incident of violence in Thoreau's life, and he was not on the receiving end of it. During the first (and last) month of his career as a public school teacher, he caned six small schoolboys who were in no position to fight back. The incident occurred just after a school board member had called him into the hall to criticize his failure to establish classroom discipline. In a snit, Thoreau selected the six victims at random and flogged them in front of the official; then he quit.*

Of course, it is the famous Night in Jail, when Thoreau was arrested for refusing to pay taxes, that brings forth the readiest association of his name with the virtue of bravery, which grants us rather neat entree to...

2. Thoreau the Radical

Thoreau rejected the poll tax because he could not countenance supporting the Mexican War. He appeared to have great hopes for a longer stay in jail and the attendant publicity until

---

* The most courageous aspect of the episode may be the fact that he kept living in the same small town while those boys grew up. Trick-or-treating must have been an intense occasion every year for the Thoreau household.

a meddling relative paid the tax and got him sprung. As it turned out, the only reason he had to spend even the single night in lockup was the Concord jailer's decision to go home early for dinner. Had his aunt rustled up the cash a bit more efficiently, the Night in Jail would have been reduced to the considerably less inspiring Lazy Midsummer Afternoon in Jail.

"He went to gaol for the sake of his principles and suffering humanity. His essay has, therefore, been sanctified by suffering," gushed Gandhi after reading *Civil Disobedience.* "Here, in this courageous New Englander's refusal to pay his taxes and his choice of jail rather than support a war that would spread slavery's territory into Mexico, I made my first contact with the theory of nonviolent resistance," echoed Martin Luther King, who presumably skimmed right past Thoreau's remarks on the virtues of chastity and tamping down one's appetites.

Thus, in the long run Thoreau would get everything he wanted out of The Night in Jail™ PR-wise; but those who knew him personally weren't so impressed. Emerson thought the whole business silly and unoriginal: others had already done it with bigger amounts of tax unpaid and uglier potential consequences.

More to the point, Concord in the mid-nineteenth century wasn't so much like Birmingham, Alabama in the Sixties or Amritsar under the Raj as it was Mayberry under the Sheriff Andy Taylor regime. And Thoreau's jail time was only slightly longer and less comfortable than that of fellow small-town miscreant Otis Campbell, Mayberry's self-incarcerating town drunk. Years later, among Thoreau's deathbed well-wishers in Concord would be one Sam Staples, the jailer, who perhaps fretted that his negligence those many years before had somehow abetted the tuberculosis that was killing his odd friend. Floyd the barber and Goober served as pallbearers.

It appears that Thoreau ignited King and Gandhi the same way he had once ignited a whole forest: inadvertently, and with no inkling of the energy he was setting loose.

—¤—

During the turbulent 1850s, Thoreau aligned himself increasingly with the abolitionist movement of which Emerson was also an adherent. The Fugitive Slave Act, which compelled Northerners to return runaway blacks to their Southern owners, incensed them both. (And there's no rule that says wussies can't get incensed.)

As his contribution to the cause, Thoreau composed a lecture denouncing the Act, and proceeded to deliver the talk forcefully to Massachusetts audiences already inclined to agree with him. "Rather than [obey the fugitive slave law] I need not say what match I would touch, what system endeavor to blow up—but as I love my life, I would side with the light, and let the dark earth roll from under me," he thundered, boldly spewing pyromaniacal metaphors in front of nonplussed neighbors who still remembered him primarily as a bumbling setter of forest fires.

One result of this abolitionist jag was that Thoreau became much enamored of the homicidal madman John Brown, whom he met on a couple of occasions between Brown's rise to fame in Bleeding Kansas and his gory attack on Harper's Ferry. When most of Brown's supporters abandoned him after the latter episode, Thoreau composed an impassioned talk called "A Plea for Captain Brown" in which he dealt at length with the virtue of courage. This lecture had the immediate effect of boosting Thoreau's self-esteem while Brown's hanging went on as scheduled.

Shortly after the execution, a certain Francis J. Merriam—an accomplice of Brown's in the Harper's Ferry insurrection who had eluded capture—showed up in Concord. His radical allies gave him an alias and enlisted Thoreau to take him to the station and put him on a train for Canada—but without doing Thoreau the courtesy of telling him who the fellow really was, because—well, this was Thoreau, after all. Fifty-fifty chance that he'd up and set the poor chap ablaze if he got too wound up.

And since that escapade marked the apogee of Thoreau's radical activism, let's move on to…

3. Thoreau the Cooze Hound

Here is a complete chronology of Thoreau's remarkable career as a lothario:

1833	Enters Harvard at age sixteen, forty-six years before the establishment of Radcliffe.
1837	Graduates Harvard with virtue intact.
1839	Meets Ellen Sewall, daughter of an area minister. Experiences curious tingling sensation in loins. Ignores it.
1840	Unable to silence clamorous loins, sends goofy, impenetrable letter to Ellen proposing marriage somewhere along about page six; is rejected.
1841	Sprouts trademark rabid-lynx-like neck-beard thing in belief that it makes him a babe magnet. Years of nonsuccess later, it will inspire fellow Transcendentalist Louisa May Alcott to confide to Emerson that the growth would "most assuredly deflect amorous advances and preserve the man's virtue in perpetuity."
1844	Burns down forest. Female population of Concord area unimpressed.
1856	Meets, and is grossed out by, Walt Whitman.
1857	In aftermath of *Walden* success, acquires cute, open-minded, twenty-year-old groupie. Does nothing.
1862	Dies a virgin.

All right then, so women didn't rev his engines. Nor did men. The Jeffersonian diet of Eurobabes and underage mulattos would most assuredly have had no effect on him; ditto Japanese concubines. Even the estimable mojo of the January 1969 *Playboy* presumably would have left him cold. And yet he wrote at twenty-one, "Passion and appetite are always an Unholy land in which one may wage most holy war," so surely *something* was giving him night-sweats. Just what was it?

Thoreau's more besotted modern fans would answer Nature, what with all his chitchat about his "intercourse" with it, but come on. It's hard to sustain a decent chubby over such an amorphous concept. Even for a Transcendentalist.

— ¤ —

I have a theory. Would you like to hear it? Brace yourself: This is going to set Thoreau scholarship on its ear. On its ear, I tell you.

You see, there was one very special type of human encounter that Thoreau always appeared to relish and would never pass up an opportunity to experience. No, really, dude: Are you ready for this?

Here's the thing: I think Thoreau's fetish, the thing that threw him into high gear, was...*dead bodies*.

— ¤ —

Okay, okay. Sorry. Ought not to spring something like that on a person, I know. But you're getting the wrong idea. I'm not suggesting that Thoreau, you know, *did* anything with the bodies. He seems to have limited himself to just looking at them and, above all else, *describing* them.

Perhaps if he had lived longer he would have moved to the next stage. A man's most disgusting perversions tend not to emerge until well into middle age. Personally, I didn't enter my Rolling Fella Bomber phase till my late forties.

But getting back to Thoreau and his dead bodies, here's a case in point:

In 1850, news reached Concord that a ship carrying one of the original Transcendentalists home from Europe had broken up before reaching port. Emerson dispatched Thoreau, who sped to Long Island and stayed four days waiting for the woman's corpse to wash ashore. When a corpse did appear (whether *the* corpse or not was impossible to tell by then), he excitedly wrote that the body…

…*was as conspicuous on that sandy plain as if a generation had labored to pile up a cairn there… It reigned over the shore. That dead body possessed the shore as no living one could.*

Now, this particular incidence of ghoulishness can, I think, be overlooked. In her capacity as editor of the Transcendentalist journal, the missing party had once rejected an article of Thoreau's, so any writer can sympathize with his ardent desire to set eyes on her rotting carcass. That one's a mulligan. But this was neither his first "intercourse" with the dead, nor would it be the last.

The previous year he had traveled to Cape Cod with his longtime frenemy, the poet Ellery Channing. Here, too, a shipwreck occurred, so they fortuitously arrived just in time to see the bodies wash up. One can fairly hear the saliva boiling over Thoreau's tongue as he writes:

…*many marble feet and matted heads…and one livid, swollen, and mangled body of a drowned girl, to which some rags still adhered, with a string, half concealed by the flesh, about its swollen neck; the coiled up wreck of a human hulk, gashed by the rocks or fishes, so that the bone and muscle were exposed, but quite bloodless—*

All right, enough of that, now. Really, Thoreau, that will do.

These two shipwrecks in consecutive years would prove to be rare strokes of good luck for Thoreau. Thereafter, his ability to encounter drowned people would be severely hampered by the same factor that hampered his ability to meet eligible, pulse-having women, i.e. the fact that he rarely set foot outside landlocked

Concord. There were local disasters now and then, to be sure, but they were few in number and tended to be of a fiery rather than a watery nature.

The Great Concord Inferno of 1844 failed to produce a single charred human corpse—which was no doubt a relief to Thoreau, who had, let us not forget, started it. But Fortune would smile upon him in 1853 when the local powder mill blew up through no fault of his own. Thoreau sprinted forth, of course, and found to his delight bodies still strewn about that were…

…naked and black, some limbs and bowels here and there, and a head at the distance from its trunk.

He continued, in a journal entry smeared with thick globules of his own drool:

The feet were bare; the hair singed to a crisp…

—¤—

That would be it for human carnage in Thoreau's lifetime. A town has only one powder mill to give, alas. Oh, sure, the Civil War—the single most prolific generator of mangled corpses in American history—would break out just several years later, but its horrific battles would rage too far from Concord for Thoreau to rush and see, and anyway, his own tubercular body was by then on the verge of joining the Corpse Corps.

He made do as best he could. Later in the year of the powder mill explosion, he would travel to Maine with a man named Thatcher who was hot to kill a moose. When he succeeded, Thoreau gleefully described the process of skinning and butchering the animal, which we will spare the gentle reader, convinced that our case is already proven beyond a reasonable doubt.

Well, okay: one more for the road. During the pseudo-scientist phase of his later years, he became fascinated with the predatory nature of animals—the way a heron used its long beak to murder a turtle in its shell being a primary example. "Such is Nature," he quite literally exclaimed, "who gave one creature a taste or yearning for another's entrails as its favorite tidbit!!"

Such is Nature, too, that gave Thoreau the compulsion to keep trying to force the rest of us to read about such things.

4. Thoreau the Writer

Our diametrically opposing views on the supposed unholiness of Passion and Appetite notwithstanding, I must confess that I identify more strongly with Thoreau than with any of the other distinguished wussies we have met. Not only are Thoreau and I both wussies, after all, but we're both writers! And so much alike in so many ways. Check it out:

1. As young writers who had trouble getting our articles published, we both broke off ties with amenable magazine editors over manuscript alterations made without our permission, then spent a decade in the unpublished wilderness regretting this idiotic outburst of principled behavior. (Well, at least I did.)

2. We both have kept lifelong journals that no one should ever be forced to read, chockfull of catty remarks about our contemporaries and long, self-flagellating lamentations on our own lack of productivity.

3. We've both been known to pay to get a book into print.

4. When in our forties, we both somehow managed to acquire a cute, ardent, twenty-year-old female admirer—though only one of us handled the situation with dignity and grace. Score one for Henry.

5. We have both burned down a forest. No wait—turns out that I haven't. Score one for me.

—◻—

At this point, I can perceive hackles slowly rising on the necks, and neck-beards, of Thoreau devotees everywhere. How dare this Muggins blighter compare himself to Thoreau, they mutter darkly. Both may be writers, they might reluctantly concede (if for no other reason than that I am the one putting these words in their mouths), but there is a major distinction to be made here: Thoreau was a *good* writer.

Yes, yes, point taken. Thoreau was a far better writer than I'll ever be, as can be seen most readily via his remarkable descriptive powers. Here's Thoreau on a night in the forest:

I turn and see the silent, contemplative, spiritual moon shedding the softest imaginable light on the western slopes, as if, after a thousand years of polishing, their surfaces were just beginning to be bright; a pale whitish luster. Already the crickets chirp to the moon a different strain, and the night wind blows, rustling the leaves, from where? what gave it birth?

Now here's me, describing the atmosphere inside the fabled Rathskeller bar of Mankato, Minnesota, circa 1975—and in ostentatious second person, no less:

Your power to describe the charm of the Rat's was to be forever hobbled by the perpetual dimness of both the place itself and that of your senses through all the hours of all the nights of all the years spent therein. What it was is best left to the individual's imagination.

In other words: It was a cool bar, but it was dark and I was always drunk. So you folks, you know, should figure it out for yourselves.

Thoreau was not only a better writer than I, but a cockier one as well. Case in point: he had his first book, *A Week on the Concord and Merrimack Rivers*, printed at his own expense. I briefly considered going the same route, but the only willing printer to be found would not commit to a run of under a thousand copies and, for fear of getting stuck with more than half of them, I went the safer route of going through a Print-on-Demand firm. In fact, Thoreau's printer likewise insisted on a thousand-book run, of which fewer than three hundred sold.

Years later Thoreau was still harumphing off to surveying jobs or logging hours in the family pencil-making business to pay down that printing bill; but at least the seven hundred unsold copies lining his walls served as excellent insulation through many a harsh New England winter.

—◻—

So all you fuzzy-necked Thoreau-worshipping hooligans can back off, okay? I fully accept and acknowledge Henry's superior kung fu.

One thing still bothers me a bit, though, and that's the persisting image of Thoreau as a *pithy* writer. I suppose this arises from the many famous aphorisms he churned out. You know: "The mass of men lead lives of quiet desperation," the one about the beat of a different drummer, etc.

The thing is, when you actually wade into Thoreau's prose, you aren't blinded by the glare of all these verbal gems lying around you on every side. It's more like crawling through a pitch-dark diamond mine that's 99.9 percent soot with a few scattered glimmers in it.

Furthermore, as a stylist Thoreau shared with Jefferson a substantial phobia of the period, and went to great lengths to avoid using it. The lover of dead humans couldn't abide a dead sentence. Once he had breathed life into one, he would resort to any sort of syntactic defibrillator—the semicolon, the dash, the embedded clause, the sentence-final participle—just to keep the poor, frail thing alive for another dozen or so words. Consider this opening gambit to the chapter of *Walden* titled "Baker Farm." (I recommend packing a lunch):

> *Sometimes I rambled to pine groves, standing like temples, or like fleets at sea, full-rigged, with wavy boughs, and rippling with light, so soft and green and shady that the Druids would have forsaken their oaks to worship in them; or to the cedar wood beyond Flint's Pond, where the trees, covered with hoary blue berries, spiring higher and higher, are fit to stand before Valhalla, and the creeping juniper covers the ground with wreaths full of fruit; or to swamps where the usnea lichen hangs in festoons from the white-spruce trees, and toadstools, round tables of the swamp gods, cover the ground, and more beautiful fungi adorn the stumps, like butterflies or shells, vegetable winkles; where the swamp-pink and dogwood grow, the red alder-berry glows like eyes of imps, the waxwork grooves and crushes the hardest woods in its folds, and the wild-holly berries make the beholder forget his home with their beauty, and he is dazzled and tempted by nameless other wild forbidden fruits, too fair for mortal taste. Instead of calling on some scholar, I paid many a visit to particular trees, of kinds which are rare in this neighborhood, standing far away in the middle of some pasture, or in the depths of a wood or swamp, or on a hill-top; such as the black-birch, of which we have some handsome specimens two feet in diameter; its cousin the yellow-birch, with its loose golden vest, perfumed like the first; the beech, which has so neat a bole and beautifully lichen-painted, perfect in all its details, of which, excepting scattered specimens, I know but one small grove of sizable trees left in the township, supposed by some to have been planted by the pigeons that were once baited with beech nuts near by; it is worth the while to see the silver grain sparkle when you split this wood; the bass; the hornbeam; the* celtis occidentalis, *or false elm, of which we have but one well-grown; some taller mast of a pine, a shingle tree, or a more perfect hemlock than usual, standing like a pagoda in the midst of the woods; and many others I could mention.*

If you're keeping score at home, that's two sentences totaling three hundred and sixty-one words. Between the indent and the second period, Thoreau unleashes forty-one commas, an even dozen semicolons, about twenty different plant species, five explicit "like" similes plus at least three others in subtler garb, four mythological references, and five terms that arouse Spell Check's suspicions. Give him credit for lapsing into a dead language only once, however, as he's not often that continent.

Many are the times I have found myself hacking my way dazedly through a Thoreauvian sentence when the unwelcome appearance of an *it* or a *he* snaps me out of my torpor. *Curses*, I realize at such moments, *now I'll have to retrace my steps until I reach the antecedent.* A word to the wise: When reading Thoreau, always leave a trail of crumbs.

There are those, I suppose, who will accuse me of hypocrisy for teasing Thoreau for his long-windedness. Well, below are ten actual published lines from each of us on related themes. So let the reader decide ¿Quién es más pithy?

The Thoreau vs. Muggins Aphorism-Off

Thoreau	Muggins
Do not be too moral. You may cheat yourself out of much life. Aim above morality. Be not simply good; be good for something.	Be holy of heart and pure of mind. But check where your love hotels are located in all likely dating spots, just in case.
If you have built castles in the air, your work need not be lost; that is where they should be. Now put the foundations under them.	But the whole shebang rested on my code of ethics: a house of cards built on sand.

Men have become the tools of their tools.	[I]t should go without saying that she aroused me, in the way that only a girl who applies the Figure-Four Leg-Lock more frequently than eye shadow can.
How vain it is to sit down to write when you have not stood up to live.	One agent quoted my own cover letter back at me while suggesting helpfully (and hopefully) that I might want to actually *go* on "a harrowing tour of human nature's darkest corners" before attempting to write about one.
We are a race of tit-men.	One lady…had nipples that were as big as her face.
I should not talk so much about myself if there were anybody else whom I knew as well.	At this point, the book abandons all pretense of addressing the reader's needs and becomes all about me, me, me.
I went to the woods because I wished to live deliberately, to front only the essential facts of life, and see if I could not learn what it had to teach, and not, when I came to die, discover that I had not lived.	May the good that I have done live after me … and may the evil be tethered to my boner.

I wanted to live deep and suck the marrow out of life.	"She sucked on your fingers? At Denny's?"
The mass of men lead lives of quiet desperation.	My God, people sure are effed up.
I stand in awe of my body.	That's a god-awful lot of excess sperm.
Word Count: 171	*Word Count: 176*

Well, all right… What does that prove, anyway?

5. Thoreau the Moss-Eater

As an American writer on nature and its beauty, he was beyond compare. As an actual outdoorsman, however, he was less Meriwether Lewis than Jerry. For a naturalist, he just didn't get out all that much in his youth. And of course there was that fateful day in 1844 when Thoreau took a callow young Harvard man out fishing, then decided to build a fire to cook their catch in the middle of very dry woods on the shores of Fair Haven Bay. Goodbye, three hundred forested acres.

Frankly, I've never in my entire career written a moving description of a moonrise, or of the first signs of spring, or of a pair of battling ants. I can take or leave nature. I don't especially enjoy camping out unless it entails at least the theoretical prospect of a handjob.

For all that—I don't know, maybe it's just me—but it just sort of stands to reason that a person—call him "Writer M"—who is largely indifferent to nature but avoids burning down so much as a single acre of forest ought to be considered something of a superior environmentalist to another hypothetical person—"Writer T," let's say—who expresses a deep and abiding love for nature but burns down *three hundred* acres of the stuff. Again, I could be all wet on this.

In a journal that served as a repository for his every thought—every synaptic whisper or puffy little brainfart that ever flitted through Thoreau's head—not a single word about the fire would appear until six years after the fact. When a man wussies out even in the privacy of his own journal, my friends, that man is carrying a serious load of wussitude.

A rueful and penitent Thoreau would ultimately over-compensate for his crime, devoting much of the last decade of his life to scientific inquiries into the evolution of plants and the distribution of trees. He even became the first person of any note to advocate setting aside land for national parks. Call him America's Moss-Eater-in-Chief.

Exactly ten springs after the forest fire, he was out in the woods taking painstaking notes on the precise timing of the leafing of trees and shrubs and the opening of flowers. "We are related to *all* nature, animate and inanimate," he had written by then. "A pine wood is as substantial and as memorable a fact as a friend." All well and good, but as far as we know he never set fire to any of his friends—some of whom, frankly, were starting to deserve it more than the forest ever did.

—¤—

As with Hirohito, one comes to suspect that Thoreau's pro-nature stance was to some extent an anti-human one at heart. But Thoreau didn't want to evade humans altogether the way Hirohito did. For one thing, Thoreau loved to argue, and humans tend to make nimbler adversaries in debate than, say, bullfrogs or red squirrels. Besides which, humans were both the possessors and main producers of the most tantalizing dead bodies around.

"I think that I love society as much as most, and am ready enough to fasten myself like a bloodsucker for the time to any full-blooded man that comes in my way," he writes ominously at the outset of the "Visitors" chapter of *Walden*. But a few chapters later, he offers this disdainful appraisal of the lay-abouts who line the village streets in the daytime:

These are the coarsest mills, in which all gossip is first rudely digested or cracked up before it is emptied into finer and more delicate hoppers within doors.

But if you want to see some real gossipers, you need look no further than Thoreau's fellow Transcendentalists. We have already noted Louisa May Alcott's ungenerous remarks, made behind Thoreau's back to Emerson, on the former's neck-beard fashion statement. Nathaniel Hawthorne cut to the heart of the matter more succinctly, describing Thoreau as "ugly as sin, long-nosed, queer-mouthed."

Then there's the whole Emerson-Thoreau relationship, so widely idealized as a sort of mentor-mentee bromance, but which upon closer examination resembles nothing so much as the mutually confounding bond between Jed Clampett and his dewy-eyed nephew Jethro.

Emerson never quite got his younger friend. In later years he wrote of Thoreau, "I fancy it an inexcusable fault in him that he is insignificant here in the town. He speaks at Lyceum or other meeting but somebody else speaks and his speech falls dead and is forgotten." To Emerson, Thoreau was an underachiever, a slacker, always wasting time on some harebrained scheme or other. You can almost picture Emerson shaking his head slowly and drawling, "Someday I'm gonna have a *loooooooong* talk with that boy."

And this is not to cast Thoreau as a naïve bystander in this catty coterie. He used to enjoy daily walks with his best bud Channing, then go home and trash the poet in his journal for his vulgar jokes and slipshod writing. At one point Thoreau wrote that—get this, now—Channing ought to be forced to write in Latin as a means of upgrading his grammar skills. In *Latin!!*

No! you may well gasp. *OMG! No, he didn't!*

But oh, yes! Yes, he *did!*

—¤—

I believe that water is the only drink for a wise man; wine is not so noble a liquor; and think of dashing the hopes of a morning with a cup of warm coffee, or of an evening with a dish of tea! Ah, how low I fall when I am tempted by them! Even music may be intoxicating… Of all ebriosity, who does not prefer to be intoxicated by the air he breathes?

At a certain point, one begins to see Thoreau's enduring appeal to college chicks. Might as well just come out and say it: He's so darned *harmless*. Oh, sure, he might randomly decide to cook fish in your garage and burn down your whole neighborhood, but at least he won't spy on you in the shower or lunge for your soft tissues in a tent in the middle of the night just to prove a point.

A girl could take Thoreau camping from coast to coast and her biggest concern would be death by tedium while listening to his endless pibble-pabble about the succession of forest trees or the varying thickness of the ice on a pond through the stages of a long winter. The man was way too interested in the dispersal of conifer seeds to be bothered with the dispersal of his own.

Modern Moss-Eaters should take note, however, of the fact that in the years immediately following the Great Concord Inferno, Thoreau's most salient action toward the forest was…well, to go out and kill even more trees. Specifically, he chopped down a number of white pines to build for himself his famous house on Walden Pond.

—¤—

And let's give Thoreau his due: clumsy as he was with women and matches, the man could wield his tools. He cut down those trees himself and put up that frame house with about as little assistance as possible. He plowed the field by the house and raised crops on his lonesome. Earlier in life, he had also constructed a seaworthy boat with his brother for their river trip.

He willed himself into a passable surveyor; he also devised a way to grind graphite that allowed his father's company to produce award-winning pencils. Personally, I have never built a house or boat with my own hands, and I got voted off *America's Top Graphite Grinder* at the regionals last year.

Having admirably completed his house and his bean field by the pond, he launched his famous experiment in self-reliance—living on freely given land little more than a mile from friends and family. As one of his biographers points out, around the same time that Thoreau was holing up at Walden, Herman Melville was off hustling cannibal chicks in the South Pacific, Sir John Franklin was sailing toward the Arctic never to return, the Mormons were setting out for an uncertain future in Utah, and the Donner party likewise was barreling westward toward less auspicious results.

Even best friend and fellow Concord wastrel Channing had rambled as far as the exotic Illinois prairie, where he had already gotten the whole build-your-own-hut-and-survive-in-it thing out of his system six years earlier. "[Thoreau] was not one to delude himself that his present abode [at Walden Pond] was actually in a wild or primitive place," the biographer notes. All well and good, but if Thoreau's peers and readers wanted to succumb to that delusion about him, he didn't seem especially keen on setting them straight.

Thoreau's two years "alone" in the Walden wilderness included the following: He went back to the family home for several weeks while the plaster dried inside the cabin. During a one-month period in 1846, he took a night off to relax in jail (which was probably cooler than the cabin on a late July night anyway), hosted a meeting of an antislavery society, and set off on a two-week excursion to the Maine woods. That's right—he took a vacation to the *real* woods to get away from the piddling suburban woods of Walden Pond.

For all that, there is no question that the man loved nature. And not just in the abstract. "I feel that I draw nearest to understanding the great secret of my life in my closest intercourse with nature," he wrote during his time on the Concord and Merrimack Rivers. And on another occasion: "If some are prosecuted for abusing children, others deserve to be prosecuted for maltreating the face of nature committed to their care."

Ladies and gentlemen, I give you Henry David Thoreau: Educator and naturalist. Flogger of random schoolchildren. Forest-fire setter. Great American wussie.

18. *Great Wussies I Have Known, Vol. 3*

Mamoru

As the early October rains gave way to Yokohama's long and glorious autumn, the murmuring among the girls of the freshman Level 2B English class for someone to step forward and organize the class *nomi-kai* inevitably rose to a clamor. It was one of those grating, nasal clamors, let it be noted, the sort of clamor that platoons of disgruntled nineteen-year-old Japanese females specialize in.

No one could say why every section of freshman English had to hold a *nomi-kai* (literally a "drinking meeting"). I had been teaching in the International Relations Department at NU since the dawn of the Nineties, a decade then nearing its end, and all I could tell you was that the custom predated my arrival, its origins lost in the mists of time. It was like the annual Lottery in the Shirley Jackson story in that sense; also in the sense that both traditions culminated in a criminal act, given that virtually all NU freshmen were under the legal drinking age.

It must have been a very old ritual indeed, since a list of bylaws as long and detailed as the Code of Hammurabi had been passed down from freshman class to freshman class. To wit:

➤ The party had to be held at an *izakaya*, that uniquely Japanese blending of bar and folksy family restaurant, and said *izakaya* had to be located either in the vicinity of NU's local train station or near the Yokohama central station. The *kanji*—party manager—would select the site and reserve a sufficient number of tables, and then lead the class into the *izakaya* en masse at precisely the designated hour.

➤ For his toast, the now solemn *kanji* would defrost some stale platitudes about establishing friendlier relations among classmates and then conclude with a bellowed *Kampai!,* upon which cue everyone would click glasses with everyone else within reach and then begin eating and drinking as if they were on a clock, which indeed they were.

➤ Sometime later a male member of the group would arrive at the conclusion—utterly lacking in successful precedent and yet tenaciously clung to—that the way to a female classmate's heart was through the shoving of chopsticks up his nostrils and the laying of circular slabs of processed fish over his eyes.

➤ At some mystic moment, seat-changing would become obligatory, so that everyone could spend part of the evening babbling drunkenly to everyone else.

➤ During that time, if the teacher drank excessively and said unprofessional things to the female attendees and expected to be forgiven for it by the next class, he would have to cough up three times the agreed-upon share of the bill.*

➤ Anyone could order anything at anytime, on the condition that the order be wailed in a piercing, nasal drone. Food-and-drink combos ordinarily too abominable to countenance would become

---

* I'm still not convinced that this was part of the original code, but it was frequently invoked in my presence.

acceptable, even laudable. Vodka cocktails were paired with raw fish. Hot Japanese saké would wash down pizza.

➤ When a participant became too impaired to find his/her way home, it would fall upon the soberest of same-sex classmates to nurse the wastrel back to health—or at least to ambulatory status. After that, it was fair play to wash one's hands of the individual with a cheery wave as he/she staggered through the station turnstiles toward certain doom.

There was one more unwritten rule worth noting: the party manager, the driving force behind the whole affair, had to be male. Nothing could get rolling until that fateful moment when an external-genital-having student stood up at the end of a class one day and muttered something along the lines of "There's been some talk of maybe us having some sort of *nomi-kai*…"

—◻—

To say the least, the class *nomi-kai* was a complicated and heavy responsibility. The freshman boys who took on the chore of organizing it were a hearty breed—young men destined to become captains of industry, political powerhouses, legal eagles, and in the shorter term, compromisers of the virtue of NU freshman girls. Alas, the Level 2B section, which I taught, included no such worthies. And that is why the leaves were falling from the cherry trees on campus with the party still unconceived.

All six other levels had already held their parties, most of them way back in the middle weeks of the spring semester, and the snooty daimyos of 2A and 3B were hinting about a second party for Christmas—an overt in-your-face to the laggards of 2B. Thus, I was getting anxious emails from the females of my class, urging me to step in and nominate a champion for them.

The pickings were slim. In a class of thirty-two souls, the male population consisted of a tall, mincing ninny, a tiny weasel with five-o'clock shadow, a pudgy and genial wussie, and a lazy, colorless dweeb. That was it. I wavered on the ninny for a while but finally settled on the wussie, who went by the name Mamoru.

He was, as I may have mentioned, pudgy, and a tad on the short side, though he towered over his friend, the weasel. Thick, arched eyebrows formed a roof of sorts over his broad slab of a face. His default expression was an uneasy parched-lipped smile.

Like most students in Level 2, the second lowest of the levels, he spoke English in a slow and deliberate manner, groping for the words he needed with visible effort, one by one, before uttering them. Unlike the others, who would pause so that the words seemed separated by ellipses, Mamoru tended to elongate his vowels to keep one word going until he could conjure up the next one. "I left my umbrella in the library" would come out...

Iiiii-leeeft-myyyyy-umbreeeeella-in-the-liiiiiibraaary.

...so that he sounded like the world's most jittery drunk.

Whenever Mamoru stood before the class with another student to perform an assigned dialogue from memory, it was my custom to sidle up next to him and run my fingers up and down his spine. This usually elicited from him a charming low gurgle, the sound of someone trying to start a car with a flooded engine, even as he gamely continued his recitation. On those occasions when it did not, I would slowly enfold him in my arms from behind and rest my chin on his soft shoulder until the desired effect was achieved.

When I sprang the good news of his nomination on him one day during writing workshop time in the computer room, he insisted that he was not a suitable choice. *Iiiiiiiim-noooooooot-suuuuuuuuitable*, he said. I told him that that was what they all said, which was true enough, except that they all said it a little more briskly. I assured him that he would do a fine job, but as insurance I asked two girls to provide covert backup.

These were Michiko, a somewhat gawky, bespectacled, and fiercely intelligent young lady who by this time was sending me long emails every night that seemed to convey every single thought that had bubbled through her head in the course of that day; and her faithful companion, the sparrow-like Yoshiko. These two chaste dork-ettes hardly seemed any more qualified than Mamoru to organize an inhibition-shedding bacchanal, but at least there would be three of them now.

And so it came to pass a few days later that Mamoru summoned the courage to stand up in class and announce his intention to organize the *nomi-kai*. This news set the sea of female heads spread out before him into a spasm of nodding, which seemed to gratify him, for he started gurgling. Meanwhile, Michiko and Yoshiko had already begun the legwork that they knew Mamoru would be too shy to do: visiting numerous *izakaya* in the area to compare their menus and glean what kind of discounts a group of our size might qualify for.

The two secret agents powwowed with their titular leader after class, and eventually a concrete proposal took form. All that remained was to sell it to the class as a whole.

—▢—

It was on Fridays that we met in the computer room, and it was on this day that Mamoru came to the front to present the class with "his" findings. In retrospect this was a costly blunder. On other days we met in conventional classrooms where he could have confronted his peers on a level playing field. In the cramped computer classroom, a teacher (or guest speaker) addressed the multitude from a high platform, a necessary device for allowing one to see the students over the tops of the enormous, boxy desktop monitors in use at the time.

Thus, from Mamoru's lofty perch, he looked down at the upper halves of his classmates' faces: twenty-eight pairs of disembodied, expectant female eyes—some batting, some shifting, most just staring.

"Next Friday, we'll meet at the station at six-thirty," he began, confidently enough, in his native language. "At seven, we'll proceed to the Laugh-Laugh Bar. We'll have a two-hour appointment. It's all-you-can-drink, and it'll be four thousand yen per pers—"

"Excuse me, did you say the Laugh-Laugh?"

"Yes, I did."

"And did you say four thousand yen?"

"Yes, I did."

The persistent questioner was one Rina, a high-strung waif with large *anime* eyes and bobbed hair and small tits.

If that last detail seems gratuitous and sexist, know that Rina herself claimed it as her trademark. Talk to Rina for any length of time, and you were certain to hear the topic of her mammaries raised and the teensiness thereof expounded upon whether you liked it or not. I first heard her bring the matter up during a small-group English discussion on the topic, "What one thing about yourself would you most like to change?" In that context, citing her modest bustline was not out of place; but thereafter it kept getting dragged into the discourse regardless of topic. "We should force North Korea to abandon its nuclear ambitions," she would assert in the heat of a debating exercise before adding, "and I have really small funbags." Memory is a tricky thing, but that's how I remember her.

"My friend's tennis club had their party at the Laugh-Laugh," Rina now reported to all present in the computer room, "and she told me that if you get the all-you-can-drink special, you can only order beer and saké."

This news sent a shock wave through the sea of monitor-veiled heads facing Mamoru. The very sort of agitated murmur (*rutabaga, rutabaga…*) that you'd think only erupts at pivotal moments in courtroom dramas now swelled throughout the room. Mamoru's mouth began to flap in a carp-like manner, but no sound emerged.

"I heard that when Class 3B had their party—I forget where—they only paid three thousand yen and they could drink anything they wanted," someone said, spurring a brief upsurge in the *rutabaga*s.

"I don't see why we should pay more and get less choice," said Rina, for once leaving her udders out of it.

"They say there's this really cool new place up by Yokohama Station," yet another girl was saying, and at this point the courtroom fell into a general convulsion for want of a Judge with sufficient gravitas to gavel them to silence. Hostile inquiries were hurled at Mamoru through the din.

I had never witnessed an actual emasculation before, and here one was unfolding before me, quite literally live and on stage. And it wasn't a single female on the attack. It was a whole pack of she-wolves going at him, taking their time, munching on extremities, working their way slowly inward toward the shriveling nutsack. A better teacher would have intervened, but I could only stand stock-still, transfixed by the spectacle. It was at this point that Michiko vaulted onto the stage.

Did I say *vaulted?* Again, memory is a tricky thing. More likely she dragged her frumpy self up there, grimacing, against her better judgment—pretty much the same way she dragged her frumpy self everywhere else she went. The bloodthirsty pack ceased its feline murmuring. Then Michiko said:

"All right, no party next Friday then. Give us another week to look into it."

There was an awed silence at this tacit admission that Mamoru had not been carrying out his *kanji* duties alone. That silence was not long-lived, however, for from the unseen mouth below the enormous round eyes of Rina came:

"But what about Mamoru's plan? Mamoru, *why* did you choose the Laugh-Laugh? And why *didn't* you—"

Michiko slouched forward, squinted, and let loose a long, pained groan that instantly cut Rina off. It was as close as one well-bred Japanese college girl can come, in discourse with another well-bred Japanese college girl, to snarling, a la Sigourney Weaver in *Aliens, "Get away from him, you bitch!"* and then turning a flame-thrower on her. It had the desired effect.

"Next week, same time," sighed Michiko. And I think she then tugged on the sleeve of the stunned and disgraced Mamoru to lead him off the stage. Then again, memory is a tricky thing.

— ¤ —

As advertised, the drama resumed the following Friday in the computer room. This time Mamoru remained seated, arms resting limply in his lap, like a sullen, defeated Buddha. I wanted to put my arms around him in hopes of jump-starting his gurgling but thought the better of it. There are times for making your male students gurgle and there are times for leaving them alone, and this was undoubtedly one of the latter.

Privately, Michiko felt as unworthy to organize the class party as Mamoru quite rightly had before her. I knew this because it was one of the major themes of her email throughout the intervening week. I tried to encourage her, but found that I had lost confidence in my ability to encourage students after the egregious gaffe of nominating Mamoru. I just told her to do her best—that I was depending on her.

This time she took the stage alone. She said, "Yoshiko and I went to twenty-two places, some around here and others downtown. The best one is this *izakaya* on the fifth floor of a building behind More's Department Store near Yokohama Station. It's three thousand five hundred yen…"

Here the murmuring crept up again, and Rina raised her hand. Michiko nipped the dissent in the bud with another squint and groan. Each squinty groan on Michiko's part was an eye-opening revelation to me. It was on that Friday morning, with the flickering fluorescents reflecting off her geeky glasses, amid the whir of thirty-two boxy Fujitsu behemoths struggling to run Windows 95, that the theretofore imperceptibly gradual process of my falling for her turned into a plunge. Dorky waters run the deepest, I then realized.

A tense silence fell over the computer classroom. Michiko, not unlike Ulysses S. Grant, slouched down and pressed ahead, undeterred by the prospect of further enemy fire.

"...It's three thousand five hundred yen, but it's all-you-can-drink *and* all-you-can-eat."

It is difficult to express the impact of the latter part of that statement on a roomful of desperately dieting Japanese freshman girls yearning for any excuse to cut loose. A standing ovation would have been a bit too much to expect at this point, but the tone of the *rutabaga*-ing had shifted from minor to major mode. And Michiko wasn't done.

"And here's the menu for you to check."

On cue, the sparrow-like Yoshiko hopped to her tiny feet and passed out photocopies. A wave of *ooh*ing and *aah*ing washed over the room as the copies flowed down the rows. Michiko's bill passed by acclamation.

—◻—

You would think that the *nomi-kai* itself would have supplied some sort of redemption for Mamoru. In a movie, that certainly would have been the case. In a movie, he would have been hit by a beer truck en route to the *izakaya* and let slip some quotable dying words like "Drink to me, drink to my health" or some such with his head lolling in the lap of the birdlike Yoshiko as he gurgled off into the Great Unknown. But this was real life, and Fate did not so accommodate him.

Make no mistake, though: the *nomi-kai* was a great success. Everyone enjoyed it and everyone gave Michiko due credit, with a pat on the noggin for Yoshiko as well. Meanwhile, Mamoru quietly got drunk in a dark corner on one and a half glasses of beer. He did not shove chopsticks up his nostrils, nor did he make any other attempts to call attention to himself. Girls left him alone all night, though there was nothing special about that. Class 2B's seven-to-one female-to-male ratio once again proved impervious to a wussitude of such magnitude.

The obligatory group photo, taken on the street outside the *izakaya* afterward, shows Mamoru lurking blurrily on the far left side, the much delighted Rina and her posse giving the V sign in the middle, and me hovering creepily against a flushed and smiling Michiko over near the right margin.

—◻—

Eventually he got over the debacle, of course. On some level he realized that he hadn't really lost face with his classmates, since he had never had any in the first place. Like wussies in similar situations throughout the world, he was destined to be liked by all his female peers, but only in the same way that they liked houseplants or elevator Muzak.

I kept in touch with Mamoru throughout his university career, of course. He, too, became a regular email correspondent. Two years later he fell for a girl, a classmate at an English conversation school that he attended outside the university, and remarkably enough he managed to ask her out to dinner—twice. And even after the second rejection he was gearing up for a third assay when he spotted said girl at Yokohama Station engaged in extremely friendly discourse with another boy from the same English school.

Later that evening I read his panicked report ("I doubted my eyes. Why!! Why!!") two-thirds of the way through the bottle of wine that had become my nightly constitutional in those days. "What if she has already had intercourse?" Mamoru cyber-blubbered.

Around this time, some of my own most valued relationships (e.g. that with Michiko) were developing, as Hirohito would have couched it, not necessarily to my advantage—hence the nightly bottle of wine—and I was in no mood to help someone with problems even more inane than my own. But I sucked it up and gave it my best shot. "Keep yourself busy, focus on other things, and something good will come to you sooner than you expect," I wrote back in a rare synthesis of responsible, adult-like behavior and fortune-cookie wisdom.

I'd like to believe that that prediction held up, but if so it didn't happen during his university years, after which I lost track of him.

Good grief. *What if she has already had intercourse?* Could anyone better encapsulate the sum of all wussie fears in seven little words?

Someday, I thought at the time, I'll have to teach him not to say such things out loud.

19. The Terminal Wussie

All the ingredients of life that wussies find so terrifying—demanding bosses, contact sports, airport security, airports, air—can be circumvented indefinitely with sufficient planning, save one. Hint: It's not taxes.

Wussies die a thousand times before their deaths, Shakespeare noted; the Valiant never taste of death but once. This has always struck me as an acutely unfair division of labor considering how much better equipped the Valiant are for this whole nasty dying business.

I suppose that pretty much everyone's a wussie when the topic of long-term suffering and pain comes up, the only difference being that the true wussie defines "long-term" as anything exceeding the prick of a flu shot. And he dreads that inevitable sit-down with a doctor that culminates in the Very Bad News even more than others do.

In John Wayne's final vehicle, *The Shootist*, the aging Duke portrays aging western gunman J.B. Books, who learns that he has prostate cancer from a doctor played by the even crispier Jimmy Stewart. (We are spared the actual examination scene.) "You have a *cancer! Advanced!*" Jimmy trills, jowls flopping in all their bad-poetry-reciting-on-Johnny-Carson fury. Subsequently, he unspools for J.B. the coming attractions:

Th—there'll be an increase in the severity of the pain in your lower spine, y-your hips, your groin… The pain'll become un-bear-able. No drug will moderate it. If you're lucky, you'll lose consciousness, but until then y-y-you'll scream.

"Now-now-now, this is not advice. It's not even a *suggestion*," Doctor Jimmy concludes as he sends Books off with a bottle of liquid opium. "It's just something for you to reflect on while your mind's still clear… *I would not die a death like I just described.*"

The remaining two-and-a-half acts of the movie, then, consist of the Duke's character groping for a quicker, more cinematic way out. It appears that Doctor Jimmy's hint that he should off himself was not too opaque for him. He does have access to guns—his character is "The Shootist," after all—and his gigantic head is an easy enough target, so one would think that a solution would readily present itself.

But this is the Duke, so you know right away that he's not going to take that route. Nor is he going to chug opium like a hippie until the cancer gets the better of him. People aren't going to line up at the box office to hear a drooling, bedridden Duke murmur, "I'm gonna ride the whipsaw over to the wishing well, Pilgrim" or some such feverish drivel as his sign-off.

No, he aims to get himself shot in a barroom gunfight with a no-account polecat. No, wait—not Duke-alicious enough. Make it *three* no-account polecats. And more specifically, he aims to first get himself winged in the shoulder of his non-gunholding hand once more for old times' sake so that he can do that awkward, ill-timed twitch of his and clench his teeth to signify renewed determination after a painful setback.

Then he will finish off his adversaries one by one through a combination of guile and steely nerve, only to be shot twice in the back by a cowardly bartender, who will then in turn be shot dead by the callow Ron Howard, to whom the Duke has become the father he never knew, and into whose eyes the Duke will stare lovingly as the life flows out of him, taking with it the painful memories of all the death and violence that he has wrought and that of Jimmy Stewart's gnarly old finger blazing a trail up his birth canal, while the audience silently nods its approval.

Yes, yes, it's about time for the Duke to go, and when he goes, he's going to go that way.*

—¤—

Wussies, of course, are apt to be much less resolute in the face of the Very Bad News than a John Wayne character.† "An increase in the severity of the pain"—these are not words we can bear to hear, or even to type. I had to copy-and-paste them there just now. We don't handle death or dying at all well, no matter whose it is. Spot the Lobster's steamy demise still haunts me, tasty though he was. Even the passing of cockroaches can unnerve me.

I once found five of them of various sizes trapped in a sticky-bottomed roach motel I had planted under my refrigerator, very much alive, antennae twitching wildly. You could feel the rage emanating from four of them toward the fifth, and boy, did I know how that guy felt. Not specifically the feeling of leading a whole group to death by slow starvation, but of letting my people down—getting everyone's recess cancelled, for example.

I couldn't stand by and let this suffering continue. How would it feel to have six itchy armpits and be unable to get at any of them? So God help me, I shot several squirts of dishwashing liquid in there and…. The rest was silence.

---

* No one asked, but here is a complete transcript of that climactic scene:
  Blam!… Blam!…Blam!-Blam!… Blam!…Blam-blam! Blam!
No-account Polecat 3: *Arrr-gaargh kill you, raargh-gaargh for Alll-berrrrt!*
  Blam!…………………………………………………… Blam!
Ron Howard: *Look out!*
  Blam! Blam!…. Blam! Blam! Blam!
  Fade to black.
† For that matter, John Wayne was apt to be less resolute in the face of the Very Bad News than a John Wayne character.

Human wussies in a similar situation, alas, can hardly hope for a benevolent giant to come along and squirt instantly fatal household cleansers all over us. The human wussie's initial reaction to the Very Bad News, then, would be to hope for a natural disaster to intervene.

For those of us who live in a major earthquake zone like the Tokyo-Yokohama area of Japan, this is a far more promising scenario than the Squirting Giant. Around here, we can always hope for the onset of massive tremors followed by three or four seconds of panic, followed quickly by the arrival from on high of a massive chandelier or concrete slab—body-mangling devices sure to delight any Thoreau types who might be lurking nearby—before we know what's what. But that scenario carries two major flaws:

➤ You can never get a massive natural disaster when you need one.

➤ Even if you could, it would take out a considerable chunk of the not-yet-terminally-ill public along with you. And if you're that gentle type of soul who feels guilty about boiling lobsters or trapping cockroaches, imagine how that would make you feel on your way to the Void.

—◻—

So once you rule out timely catastrophes and mythical giants, the terminal wussie's next best option is to induce somebody to kill him quickly and painlessly.

Not three no-account polecats who need killing themselves, the way J.B. Books did it. Most of us wussies don't even know three no-account polecats well enough to invite them to a barroom gunfight with any hope of success. I can only think of two bona fide polecats that I have any truck with nowadays, neither of whom responds to my email. No, what we need is not a Polecat Mod

Squad but a single Good Samaritan, an Angel of Death. Someone to do our dirty work for us.

Happily, a two-word phrase has entered the language in my lifetime which surely appeals to any wussie who has contemplated the Long Goobye: Assisted Suicide. If this idea continues to catch on, the terminal wussie gets to have his cake and eat it too, plunging-forth-into-the-great-unknown-wise. By the time most of us Baby Boom wussies are planning our end games, the heavy lifting will be on someone else and all we'll have to do is provide the Go signal—which, of course, ought to be clarified in advance by way of a Living Will.

I don't need to tell readers astute enough to buy this book just how important a Living Will (aka Advance Health Care Directive) is, but it seems most Living Will templates don't allow the author enough opportunity for specifics. Personally, I think one needs to go beyond the basics (i.e. "Kill me.") and work out in advance a detailed system for communicating any and all needs you may have in the case of near-total incapacitation—and the less ambiguous the system, the better. If, for example, six blinks calls for changing the channel to ESPN and seven calls for immediate, painless oblivion, well, you'll only have yourself to blame for missing that crucial playoff game.

In this connection, I tried to get Mrs. Muggins to practice smothering me in case of extreme incapacitation. I whined and wheedled until she agreed to hold a pillow lightly over my face while I emitted muffled grunts and flailed spasmodically like Glenn Beck. As part of the bargain, she was supposed to remove the pillow after I went limp and gaze upon my slack-jawed, white-eyed death mask, but I couldn't really tell if she did this or not, what with my eyes rolled up to the tops of the sockets.

This was all intended quite sincerely to get her used to the harsh realities that she could face when the time comes, but she refused to rehearse with me more than the one time, muttering instead some nostalgic lament for the days when we used to have fun in bed. No doubt she'll get more into the spirit of the thing when she finds the Rolling Fella Bomber in the back of the sock drawer.[*]

—◻—

Living Wills and Assisted Suicide are all well and good but they are hardly foolproof. Most wussies realize deep down in their fluttering hearts that when the time comes, they may have to take matters into their own hands. It's not the proper office of a spouse or a friend or even the family cat, willing though she may be.

The question, then, is how. Surely almost everyone, wussie and non-wussie alike, has ticked off the options at some time or other. One wussie's list runs more or less like this:

Wussie Self-Termination Options

Method	Pros	Cons
Gunshot to head	High success rate; easy	Head much smaller than John Wayne's
Setting self aflame in public place	Excellent chance of national coverage	That would, like, really, really hurt
Hanging	Cheap and easy; a great way to get back at that belligerent janitor in your life	There's a thin line between a slow, ghastly choking death and totally gross decapitation. Just ask Saddam Hussein.

[*] I realize that I said t-shirt drawer in an earlier chapter. I have since moved it on the off chance that she might have managed to read that far.

Helium hood	Endorsed by right-to-die groups	Color-coordinating hood with beige pajamas and soon-to-be-purple face can be a nightmare.
Jumping in front of speeding train	*Whee!*	In Japan at least, kind of a cliché.
Leaping off building	Can pass it off as accident and leave heirs with life insurance payout	Wussies don't litter.
Strapping self to conveyor belt in sawmill	Will forever be the stuff of legend among adolescent nephews	As if a wussie could actually bring himself to do this.
Sleeping pill overdose	Crack open some fine wine, put on some soft music, bill the whole thing as "An Intimate Evening with Eternity"	Been there, done that.

Japanese ritual *seppuku*	Sure it's really gross and awful to slit open your own stomach, but the rules allow you a "second"— i.e., a loyal subordinate whose job it is to lop off your head before the pain gets horrific.	If you happen to *be* the second, you're SOL because by custom *you* now have to commit seppuku, too—and there's no allowance for a "third."
Suicide bomber vest	Supremely effective	Gear not readily available at Home Depot outlets

I'm sure I'm not the first wussie to long for the suicide bomber vest option, but personally I really like it. A smart marketer would arrange for the mass production of these items—assorted colors and a range of sizes would be nice, since the soon to be terminally ill wussie boomer population is skyrocketing by the minute and we're a vain lot—and bundle them with inflatable life rafts so that the terminal wussie can row himself a safe distance from shore, pull the tab, and, well: no muss, no fuss, no funeral or burial expenses.

All this idea lacks is a new name for the "life" raft.

—◻—

Of course, just how a wussie faces his imminent departure from the world depends in no small part on his faith. An upbeat and sincere belief in an afterlife, replete with harps or virgins or raisins or what have you, can go a long way to ease even the wussiest of supplicants through the door. A belief in reincarnation will do in a pinch.

Alack for me, I'm stuck with the strong suspicion that this one visit to earth is all that we get: there's nothing before or after it. It's that special. I look at human existence the way high school girls look at Prom: It's a one-shot deal and I want everything about it to be as perfect as possible. I want to enjoy it from start to finish, to create a perfectly smooth and glossy pearl of enjoyment that will shimmer for ages to come. Preferably with an under-the-sea theme. And I want the people around me to enjoy their Prom as well, of course, but perhaps just an itty-bitty little sliver less than I enjoy mine.

But a wussie's capacity for enjoyment is always limited by his fear of the end. How, then, have notable wussies faced the final curtain? It should go without saying that of the illustrious wussies featured in this book—Isaac, Hirohito, Thomas Jefferson, Henry David Thoreau—not a single one died violently in a barroom. All four left this world quietly, as if on tip-toe, of natural causes and at a mean age of ninety-eight-and-a-half.

Isaac, so far as we know, died as he had lived—passively. At one hundred eighty, he had broken his loony father's longevity record for patriarchs of that era by five years. So he had that triumph to comfort him as he faced his obscure end and... Well, pretty much just that. As for Hirohito, well, his ignominious demise at eighty-seven and its aftermath need not be revisited, I hope.

Thomas Jefferson's departure at age eighty-three from chronic diarrhea and urinary tract problems was only slightly less undignified than Hirohito's. Tradition holds that he clung to life to see the fiftieth anniversary of the Declaration of Independence.*

Accounts suggest that Jefferson was ready to go after his long illness. He knew that, half in spite of and half because of his colossal wussitude, he had left his mark on the world. Indeed, his legacy today far outshines that of John Adams, the latter's seven-

---

* I still say he clung to life till he could think of something catty to say about Madison.

part HBO bio notwithstanding, and his words live on today on the lips of Third World freedom fighters and Tea Party numbskulls alike.

—◻—

Of all our great wussie forebears, it is Thoreau who provides the model that future terminal wussies should seek to emulate. Dying of tuberculosis at just forty-four, he alone of this group had the right to feel cheated, yet he betrayed no sign of any such bitterness.

As Thoreau lay dying, he asked that his first book, *A Week on the Concord and Merrimack Rivers*, be read to him. Let me confess here that I could not finish this book. (I gather it's sort of like *Deliverance* without the bows or arrows or banjos, or cornholing, or anything else remotely of interest to anyone.) The balance of opinion among those who have finished it seems to hold that this was a book that ended up being self-published for very valid reasons. Thoreau's contemporaries didn't much care for it, either (not that the backbiting weenies would say so to his face, mind you).

It seems that whether he realized it or not, Thoreau had really written this story of the boat trip he had taken with his beloved brother in the flower of their youths for himself. He went into debt to have it published and thereafter was stuck with hundreds of unsold copies, but he had never stopped being the book's biggest fan.

His books were his babies; he loved them equally but in different ways, and for both their virtues and their flaws; and you know what? I can so relate to that.

Anticipating one of his favorite segments, Thoreau interrupted his sister to say, "Now comes good sailing," then smiled, then died. Way to go, bro.

20. Wussies and Drama Club:

A Two-Act Play

Act 1: My Daughter Emily

"I never felt so alone in my whole life," my daughter Emily is saying. "I wish I were dead! Papa! Papa!"

That's my cue. I rise and make my way upstage to comfort her. "Emily! Emily! Now, don't get upset."

"But Papa, I don't *want* to get married," she bleats, wrapping her arms around my neck.

"Shhh, Emily," I say, folding her into my arms. "Everything's all right."

Inwardly, heart racing, knees knocking, vision blurring, I'm wondering if *all right* quite sums up the current state of things. Things at this moment are simultaneously wonderful beyond description and utterly terrifying (which, I suppose, averages out to *all right*), for Ann Brown has wrapped her arms around my neck and launched a two-pronged blitzkrieg on my personal space bubble.

The hug will afterward play out in my memory in slow motion, like the video of an automobile crash test. First there is the stiff collision of the unyielding tips of Ann's bra cones against my skinny sixteen-year-old chest: my dummy-like head lolls forward on impact. Then there is the inevitable give, as her whole body propels itself into mine and those rigid cones crumple, spilling their contents in pools of warm, viscous boobage across my chest.

At the same time, my hands, reaching around her, are once again gathering data on the other side of that wondrously complex and seldom-glimpsed garment, the brassiere: the rubbery straps (one of them twisted), and the huge, cottony hump of the clasp lying under a glob of sweat.

Why is her back sweating? I wonder, idly, *It's not that hot up here on the stage*, until I remember that this glob of sweat is my own sweat, which I have deposited on the back of Ann's blouse in three installments during previous run-throughs of this Act II wedding scene. Mr. Black screeches *Cut!* and I gratefully stagger away, wiping my clammy hands on my corduroys.

There is something familiar about this odd cluster of emotions, and it occurs to me that this is not the first time a high school classmate has bushwhacked me with her unexpected womanliness. Instead of replaying the slo-mo collisions with Ann, my mind involuntarily reaches back to the first such ambush—specifically to Cheryl Von Tunzelmann's appearance in a leopard print two-piece swimsuit two weeks before we all started our freshman year of high school…

—◻—

Westhuizen had dragged me along to the high school pool for Open Swim Night on that occasion, but I deliberately left my swimsuit behind. I feared that he and the others would again spend the whole night showing off their jackknives and other fancy dives, a skill I had not yet managed to acquire. Such an eventuality would again place me in the quandary of either resorting to my limited array of pseudo-dives (the cannonball, the can-opener) or insisting that I really could dive and then trying to explain away the painful belly-flops as just another off night.

So I sat in the spectator's section, alone and fully clothed, only to find that diving would be canceled tonight in favor of horsing around in the shallow end with girls. Yes, girls were present in the pool. Girls that we had known most of our lives and yet no longer recognized, for these girls suddenly had breasts and were willing to showcase those breasts to us in two-piece swimsuits—swimsuits that you could not quite call bikinis, but that were in that ballpark.

I watched as the ruthless bully Jim Yonkman actually swam between Cheryl Von Tunzelmann's bare-naked legs and rose up out of the water with her, shrieking and yanking self-consciously at the top of her ballpark bikini, atop his shoulders. Westhuizen then did the same with Josette Oosteroom— who could not steal this scene from Cheryl but was nonetheless solid in a supporting role—and an impromptu chicken-fight broke out right there before my eyes in the shallow end: two largely undressed, breast-having classmates laughing and pawing at each other in an effort to dislodge the other from her shoulder-top perch.

It occurred to me then that my solo presence in the spectators' gallery might invite controversy, that perhaps I ought to leave, but what with the oppressive humidity of the indoor pool, the echoing of the squeals and splashes, and the heavy odor of chlorine all augmenting the effects of the two-piece swimsuits, I had no confidence in my ability to make it to the door without collapsing. Witnessing the public debut of Cheryl's womanly body was like finally spotting the long-awaited Fantastic Four *annual double-issue on the rack up at Ben's Fine Liquors. The same, yet so very different…*

Finally, both girls plunged, caterwauling, from their perches and then were underwater and out of sight for a moment, thus breaking the spell. I seized the opportunity to effect my furtive escape, and contemplated the possible impact of Cheryl Von Tunzelmann's leopard-patterned bosom on the world economy during my long stagger home.

Decades hence I would remain unable to catch a whiff of an over-chlorinated indoor pool without some degree of arousal and wooziness, and don't get me started on leopards.

—◻—

What I have just experienced on the stage of the school auditorium with Ann Brown is different, though, in a couple of ways. At the pool, Cheryl had provided only visual input. Ann, in the role of my daughter Emily, is sending my nervous system into overdrive as it attempts to process the flood of tactile data that my chest and hands are frantically dispatching re Ann's front and back sides, respectively.

A few years later, I would watch the climactic scene of *Close Encounters of the Third Kind*, in which the gigantic alien mothership spews out coded information in the form of musical tones faster than Earth's most advanced computers can process it, sending the human scientists into a panic; and I would think: *That's just like getting hugged by Ann Brown during rehearsals.*

And the tactile info is only the tip of the iceberg. There is the scent as well, a mixture of some sort of lemony shampoo and an antiperspirant fighting a losing battle against sweat that is at least in part her own, a sweet-and-sour combo platter of odors in which Sweetness triumphs while Sour's presence is oddly welcome.

There is the sight of Ann, too, the older girl whom I had always thought of as being taller and sturdier than me suddenly, magically shrinking when she enters my space bubble to the size of someone who could credibly be the grown daughter of the middle-aged newspaper publisher that I portray, or, in yet another make-believe universe, my girlfriend. She fits as neatly into my embrace as her missile-contoured yabboos fit into that formidable space-age brassiere of hers.

There are, too, the filaments of her long auburn hair that float in the air when I exhale hard on them from the force of the hug. The impact that Ann's hug brings to bear on my senses—the senses of a lad who has hugged no female but his grandmother since hitting puberty—is unfair in its sheer magnitude and in the sophistication of its weaponry.

If we were actors of the Strasberg School, then I would be too deeply immersed in my character to harbor such feelings toward my own "daughter"—or else would experience intense self-loathing over them. But we are not of the Strasberg School. I suppose we are, by default, of the Black School instead.

"Emily," mewls Mr. Black, whose directing philosophy includes addressing actors by their character's names, "the hug simply isn't convincing. This is a very emotional moment for you. It's your wedding day, you're just out of high school, you're not sure you want to go through with it. All of that has to come through, okay?"

"Okay."

"Let's block it out right now while I read through it. Mr. Webb: 'Emily, now don't get upset.' Now you hug him hard... Good, good! Like that!"

Dr. Gibbs and his son George, milling around off stage, are looking at us. I make goo-goo eyes at them. Emily tenses up.

"You pull back now, Emily, and say 'But papa,' et cetera, et cetera, 'Let's go away,' et cetera, et cetera, up until 'I'll work for you, I could keep house.' Then your father says 'Shhhh, you mustn't think of such things.' As soon as you hear that *Shhhh*, you hug him hard again and lay your head on his right shoulder... Yes, the right shoulder, yes, like that."

Again I project the *hubba-hubba* eyes to the lads off stage, causing Dr. Gibbs to chortle and Emily to break character.

"What do you do that for?" says Ann in a decidedly unfilial tone.

"Wh-what do you mean?"

"Making stupid faces. Don't deny it. Why do you have to mess around like that, treat everything like a stupid joke?"

"I don't know what—"

I look to Mr. Black for help, but he is speechless at this onslaught.

"You're such a good actor, you know that? That's what bugs me about it," she says, in a voice that is half reaching out, half pushing away.

Later I will dissect this statement, will find in it the embedded compliment and the good intentions. All too late. Right now I have to extract myself from this unpleasant situation, but being at this age still torn between pursuit of careers as an annoying twit or a harmless wussie, all I can think to do is to make goo-goo eyes at Ann, prompting her to ball her fists, shake her head violently, emit a sharp warble of exasperation, and stalk away.

As she does so I notice that small areas of the back of her blouse have been so saturated with my sweat as to render them transparent. Her brassiere is pale green, I marvel, adding one more byte to the data overload.

—◻—

If it was strange for me to be dealing with these feelings, it was even stranger to be dealing with them with regard to Ann Brown. Cheryl Von Tunzelmann, she of the leopard-print quasi-bikini, had authored many such swoons. All the boys in our class had adored her forever. I for one had been obsessed with Cheryl Von Tunzelmann's breasts before they even existed.

But Ann Brown had always been that plain, one-year-older girl from two blocks up the street who walked past my house on her way to school. She was always flanked on one side by the large and aggressively ugly Marna Lutz and on the other by the blonde, freckled cutie-pie, Janey Wouterson. If you caught them from the right angle, they suggested one of those Ascent of Man science-room posters with Ann representing the intermediate stage of human evolution between the knuckle-dragging ape and homo sapiens.

The analogy is imperfect, though, in that it was the middle figures in those illustrations that were always the most fascinating ones (good old homo erectus, or whatever he was called, still with the chimp-like head and yet walking just as upright as a game-show host), whereas plainness in a girl can hardly compete with sunny cuteness or brutal ugliness for a young man's attention.

Anyway, I always avoided those three. Deep down, there lurked a vague memory of being forced at around age five to attend a birthday party at one of their homes where they had toyed with me as if I were Pip and they a three-headed Estella.

After fourth grade Janey Wouterson moved away. This event had two lasting effects: (1) Her breasts would forever remain hypothetical to Mortonville boys, and (2) I would quickly lose all interest in watching her two friends walk past my house. Thus, my thoughts about Ann Brown over the last four or five years had been as nondescript as her name. My memory file on her would have boiled down to this:

✓   one year ahead of me

✓   honor roll regular

✓   Lutz sidekick.

She was one random blow to my head by the likes of Jim Yonkman away from getting knocked out of my hard drive once and for all.

And then along comes Mr. Black, casting me and her as father and daughter in Our Town, *literally propelling us together in a series of chest-on collisions. With the first of those double-barreled jabs to my ribcage, the long-transparent Ann suddenly leapt into three-dimensional reality. Hey, look: she has freckles just like Wouterson's!*

Who knew?

— ¤ —

I am feeling bad about what has happened. When a girl makes you feel the way Ann/Emily has made me feel during those hugs—even if involuntarily—you don't want to see her stalking away from you with balled fists. That's a given.

A calmer Ann soon returns to the stage, having easily wrested assurances from Mr. Black that we will not be doing any more hugging this evening. We pick up the wedding scene just after the hugs.

"You're just nervous, Emily," I console my still fuming pseudo-daughter at arm's length. "George! George, will you come here a minute?" I say, gesturing toward the quivering sac of protoplasm that calls itself Tim Boehner.

— ¤ —

A stereotype holds that the theater, regardless of locale, attracts gay males in disproportionate numbers, and our school did not defy that stereotype: Dean Bleekemolen leaps to mind, and possibly Zach Geingob as well.

But even if Zach qualified, a two-man play would have been about all we could have staged with an all-gay cast, and Dean and Zach had already done one. A school district our size simply couldn't generate homosexuals in the quantity and quality needed to produce large ensemble pieces on the scale of Our Town, *so the cast had to be filled out with the next best thing, wussies. That's where I came in.*

For me, high school theater held little allure in and of itself, but having failed at sports I needed something to pass the time for four years until, like generations of wussies before me, I could head for college somewhere out of state and launch my doomed bid at identity reinvention. Oh, when that glorious day came that I could cast off the shackles of wussitude and be My True Self! Until then, I had to play out the clock with the identity with which I had been unfairly saddled since quitting freshman football.

In the end, theater served its purpose. The boys who showed up for tryouts made me feel relatively macho—no one more so than Tim Boehner, a sophomore ingénue. Tim had a pasty complexion and bright red lips, which made him look like the black sheep of the Joker family, the one too timid to mastermind madcap criminal capers. Pretty much too timid for anything at all, really. Timid may well have been his given name. His presence at tryouts seemed something of a miracle, or perhaps his widowed mother's idea.

She and Tim had moved to town just that summer, when Mrs. Boehner became our school counselor in place of the chronically unpleasant Mrs. Bodwell. That retired worthy's term in office had been an odd one, since the primary duty of a counselor is to calm traumatized students, and Mrs. Bodwell herself was one of our town's leading generators of trauma. A sort of Catch-22 for Mortonville's traumatized teens, to employ a cliché not yet hackneyed at the time.

The widow Boehner was a balm on the troubled waters Mrs. Bodwell left in her wake. There was something of the mythical nineteenth century schoolmarm about her in her prim lacy collars and full-length skirts and unplucked eyebrows and gentle smile. My friend Penniman and I, who had her for study hall, ruminated on how we wished we had problems just so that we could be counseled by her. This was, in retrospect, an ironic attitude, in that we actually had loads of problems that we failed to recognize as such. At some point we had simply convinced ourselves that high school was a four-year streak of incredibly bad luck, our personal Dust Bowl, the will of fickle Gods, and that our misery was unrelated to any personal delusions or failings.

"You know, Tim really looks up to you," Mrs. Boehner remarked one day as we chatted at her desk. So there you had it—my role defined: by my junior year, I was not merely a full-fledged wussie in my own right, but a role model for the next generation.

—¤—

It is probably hard enough to be new in town, to be fatherless, and to have your mom at school with you all day. On top of all that young Tim has to bear the lone remaining legacy of his father's existence, a surname pronounced *bawner*, veritable manna for any high school's lazy nickname coiners.

He roams the halls alone, stoop-shouldered, clutching his books to his chest, always bearing the demeanor of someone whose life has just seconds earlier been very credibly threatened. Quite possibly it has been; it is that sort of high school. The least I can do for my shivering acolyte is to brighten the few hours of the evening that we share practicing *Our Town* in the auditorium.

"George, are you planning to raise chickens on your farm?" I, in Mr. Webb mode, ask him.

"What?"

"Chickens! You know—little yellow muthahs?"

"Cut!" screeches Mr. Black, as Tim begins retching all over the imaginary kitchen table. At least, that is my initial fear based on his spasms and the sickly sounds emerging from his throat. Gradually I realize that this is how he laughs.

We will go on to amuse ourselves by ad libbing our lines for the remaining weeks of practice as Mr. Black grows increasingly apoplectic. As documented in Chapter 11, Mr. Black is not having a good year at all. By day freshman boys are running roughshod over him in English I, provoking parents to complain about his Thoreauvian ineptitude at classroom management.* By night he has to watch his tenuous grip on the fall drama production slip slowly away from him and into the hands of a confederacy of wussies.

In the meantime, shy, stuttering, insecure "Boner" is gradually gaining the confidence and élan he needs to portray shy, stuttering, insecure George Gibbs with conviction while I, of course, am superb in the small role of Mr. Webb which the incompetent Mr. Black has assigned me, failing to see the natural Stage Manager within.

In idle moments during nightly rehearsal, I think how cool it would be to set up some sort of International Society of Mr. Webbs so that all of us former high school *Our Town* actors from around the world could have annual conventions, the way that there are such gatherings for guys named Bill Jones or whatever, and then, in still idler moments, I think: No it wouldn't. Be cool, that is. In fact, that just might be the uncoolest idea that anyone has ever thought of in the history of human ideas. Such are the fancies that romp through one's mind in the midst of a long weeknight rehearsal mismanaged by a sputtering nincompoop.

—◻—

The cast is running through one of the cemetery scenes while I have the above reverie. It's the part of the play in which the Grover's Corners dead sit in rows of folding chairs and robotically reflect on their lives. A nameless dead couple—in life, a farmer and his wife—have the following desultory exchange:

Wife: It's on the same road we lived on.

Farmer: Ayuh, right smart farm.

---

* I read all about it in the School Board minutes that my father left lying around, always wishing he had only been so cavalier with that *Playboy*.

In what he surely deems a clever ploy on his part, Mr. Black has cast the offspring of actual Mortonville-area farmers in these small, ghostly roles, but on this night the typecasting blows up in his face when the bowl-headed youth can't quite manage to pronounce *Ayuh*.

"Ah-*hyuhh!*" says Mr. Black.

"*Ayy*-uh!" counters the farm youth.

"It's just the way people said *yeah* in that part of the country at that time. Think of it as just a plain old *yeah* with a little *uh* in front of it."

"*Ayy*-uh!"

"Ah-*hyuhh!*"

"*Ayy*-uh!"

Compared with the farm youth, at least, Boner has range. He is my stuttering son-in-law this time out, will be the stuttering young neighbor of my aging war profiteer in *All My Sons* the following year, then stuttering Bob Cratchit to my Scrooge in *A Christmas Carol*. Small wonder he sees me as a father figure; Lord knows all the directors do. The median age of all my characters will hover in the low sixties; that of Tim's around twenty-five.

I watch Boner prostrating himself before poor dead Emily on his visit to the cemetery. He prostrates so well, my boy Boner does. *Ayy-uh, right smart prostrater*, one expects the farm kid to observe, in that robotic, lifeless way that seems to come naturally to him—but Farm Kid misses the cue.

Ann Brown, of course, never misses a cue, never blows a line, never fails to hit the right emotional pitch. "Do any human beings ever realize life while they live it? Every, every minute?" she asks the Stage Manager.

"No," replies Dean Bleekemolen, "the saints and poets maybe, they do some."

This line annoys me even more than the fact that it is Dean and not I who gets to say it. Why the saints and poets? What makes them so special? Every night after rehearsal I vow to start realizing life while I live it, every, every minute, just to show that old gasbag

Thornton Wilder how full of shit he is, but it's hard. It's hard, for example, to realize life while gang-showering with the Future Felons of America after PE. Could the poets? Could the saints? They probably got excused from PE, the weirdos.

— ¤ —

The night of our play comes at last. We sprinkle the first two acts with ad libs, get screeched at by Mr. Black during intermission, then go back out and sprinkle in more ad libs than ever. Stowing the goo-goo eyes, I hug Ann Brown hard as if for the last time ever, which, of course, it is. Afterward, she'll coolly ask me to add my comment and signature to her copy of the program and then point her perfectly congruent cones away from me forever.

Act 2: The Bravest Flee when Death Approaches

For the night of one-act plays that was the default cultural zenith of Mortonville's winter I was drafted into the piece directed by Mrs. Battersby, who, through methods all her own, had determined that our isolated little community of farmers and factory line workers and main street merchants had wearied of the steady theatrical diet of prewar farces, early Neil Simon comedies and the locust-like return of *Our Town* every seven years.

No, what these folks hungered for, though they might not realize it, was a dead Frenchman's adaptation of the third installment of a twenty-five-hundred- year-old Greek trilogy about incest, patricide, treachery, war, and self-mutilation. Ergo, she would stage Jean Cocteau's *Antigone.*

For those not up on their twenty-five-hundred-year-old Greek trilogies, here is the Antigone story in a nutshell: Boy meets Girl. Girl tries to ritually bury dead brother. King sentences Girl to death. Boy (aka Son of King) kills self. Just about everyone dies.

Now, it's certainly true that *Our Town* also had a dark side to it: as noted earlier, the whole last act takes place in a cemetery, more or less. But *Our Town*, like flu season or intramarital sex, had that air of familiarity to it that made its dreariness oddly comforting to the townsfolk.

Not so *Antigone*. With *Antigone*, theater-goers would be clubbed in the face right from the outset with the tableau of two chicks in Batgirl outfits discussing what to do with the rotting corpse of their brother, after which things go progressively downhill.

—¤—

The prospect of something as awful as the decision to put on *Antigone* happening in Mortonville was not such a stretch if one knew Mrs. Battersby, but none of us did. Who was this stout woman with the short, mannish haircut and glass-cutting voice, correctly pronouncing Dutch names from her clipboard during tryouts? Her surname gave us a hint, and indeed she turned out to be the wife of the English IV teacher, aka Mr. Battersby. Gradually we would piece together that she was a professor of English literature at a small liberal arts college in the next county.

When the cast lists were posted, I noted with envy that Miss Ford's group would be doing a delightful screwball comedy from the Forties featuring at least two roles for which I was genetically suited, a lecherous uncle and a drunk. Instead, I would be Mrs. Battersby's Hymen. Yes, Hymen. The character's name might be spelled Haemon in the script and on the program, but the audience would hear me addressed, repeatedly, as *Hymen*.

Over the next several weeks as the production took shape, a dizzying game of Good News/Bad News would unfold, as follows:

Good News: All the cast will wear masks.

Bad News: These will be teensy little Batgirl masks. Hecklers will have no trouble discerning who "Hymen" is.

Good News: Hymen represents my first (and ultimately only) role as a young, single man with a love interest.

Bad News: My love interest, Antigone, will be played by Ruth Erb, a dour senior beanpole with four inches on me.

Good News: She and I do not hug. Indeed, we have no scenes together at all. Virtually every scene in the play pivots around mighty Creon, King of Thebes, whom the other characters confront one by one. Moreover, I only have one puny little scene! In and out in five minutes tops!

Bad News: Mrs. Battersby's Cocteau-esque vision dictates that all characters are obliged to remain on stage throughout the play. When one's character is not involved in the scene, one squats down on the stage in the billowy pool of fabric formed by one's cape.

Good News: Did I mention the capes? We all get bitchin' capes in various muted autumnal colors to cover our upper bodies.

Bad News: Our legs are exposed and clad in black panty-hose. Mrs. B calls the garment *tights*, but I know panty-hose when I see it.

Good News: The lighting for the entire play will be muted by artsy blue filters for no apparent reason at all. Anything that helps obscure my identity goes in the good news column.

Bad News: Not sure I covered this yet, but my character's name is pronounced *Hymen*.

Good News: Frisky cheerleader Jerri Hackenbroch is in the cast!

Bad News: Jerri is cast in the role of Ismene, Antigone's sister. The only huggable female in the play, and my billowy cape never pools itself anywhere near hers.

Good News: You know from the get-go that Jerri will be rockin' that black panty-hose…

Bad News: …which means that pickup-truck-loads of jocks who otherwise would never have got wind of our production will be in attendance to hear me being called *Hymen*. Put all this together, and I just want to fling myself down on the stage and die.

Good News: According to Mrs. Battersby's direction, this is exactly what I do at the end of my lone scene. The act symbolizes Hymen's suicide.

Bad News: My still sentient corpse lies sprawled on a corner of the stage until the curtain falls. Which means I have to listen to Rollie Ruegsegger stumble through Creon's lines to the end of the whole god-awful enterprise.

—◻—

Here is the *Cliff's Notes* description of my scene in the play:

The father and son argue, Haemon accusing Creon of arrogance, and Creon accusing Haemon of unmanly weakness in siding with a woman. Haemon leaves in anger, swearing never to return.

It is impossible not to interject here that Rollie Ruegsegger as a father accusing me of unmanly weakness had more than a little of the old pot-and-kettle vibe to it. But that's not the point. The point is that after storming away from Creon in anger, I was to take a flying leap, belly-flop to the stage, and skid to the edge of the orchestra pit.

That wasn't exactly easy on the old ribcage. But when Mrs. B asked for six consecutive takes of belly-flopping onto hardwood, you belly-flopped onto hardwood and you liked it. You knew then that you weren't in Mr. Black's loosey-goosey Grover's Corners any more. On Mrs. Battersby's watch, you didn't compete to see who could slide the farthest across the stage in stocking feet. Needless to say, the thunder machine lost all its allure.

"*Creeeeon!*" she would scream before my corpse had even stopped skidding. "Pro-*ject!* And learn your *goddam* lines!"

That was new to us, too. Directors didn't swear at us, nor did ladies. Coaches swore at athletes, of course, but that was part of the rationale that led fellows like Boner and me to eschew sports in favor of theater.

After two weeks of rehearsal, Mrs. Battersby took me under her wing. "You're the best goddam actor in this school," she seethed. This, I knew even at the time, was a case of goddamning with faint praise, but Mrs. B. was sincere. She occasionally invited me to the nineteenth-century mansion that she shared with our inconsequential English IV teacher, where she tried to nurture a broader interest in theater in me.

At first I feared that the Battersbys were operating one of these new-fangled open marriages, and that as the evening wore on I might be led helplessly away to an upstairs boudoir replete with ceiling mirrors to further my education. Instead she simply plied me with books and spoke to me of Jean Cocteau.

At the time, I was flabbergasted by the notion that a guy had made it through high school and lived long enough to write fruity plays with the first name of a girl and a surname pronounced *Cock-toe*. That would be like Boehner to the tenth power. The unthinkable torments Cocteau must have endured in PE surely scarred him for life and warped him into the sort of freak who would think up those costumes.

So I spent several months feeling sorry for him, even though he was dead and even though while alive he had set in motion a series of events that somehow led to me being called *Hymen* in public. And just now I read on Wikipedia that in his early twenties "it was said that Cocteau could bring himself to orgasm without touching himself, purely by the power of imagination." So he had that going for him—saved him a bunch of francs on Rolling Fella

Bombas—but I wasn't aware of that at the time, and even if I had been, it wouldn't have helped me out of my predicament.

—◻—

What I did know, or at least suspected, was that we were all guinea pigs in a cruel experiment, the result of a Pygmalion-like bet between Mrs. Battersby and some hoity-toity Farnsworth College colleague.

"Anyone can be taught to perform Greek drama in a presentable fashion," I pictured Mrs. B cawing one afternoon around cocktail time as she reclined in her English-leather club chair in the Farnsworth faculty lounge and swirled her glass of claret. "*Anyone*, I say!"

"Surely you jest, Donna," I imagined her long-despised rival replying, a foot-long cigarette holder wagging between her teeth. "Would you even for a second consider staging...oh, say, Cocteau's *Antigone* with a random litter of bumpkins from one of the area high schools?" She then blows three perfect smoke rings as a mocking high-pitched titter toots from her puckered, blood-red lips. It is a laugh that Mrs. B has known and despised for years, I assume—maybe decades. And after all, who can abide a tooting titterer?

"Not only would I consider it, Hermoine," growls Mrs. Battersby, rising to her feet, "I'll let you hide in the orchestra pit during auditions and pick the goddam cast!"

And that was how we all got into this fine mess, I was sure.

—◻—

I had rung in the 1970s with Rollie Ruegsegger a few years earlier when I was a freshman and he a sophomore. We were not each other's first choice of New Year's Eve companion. I suspect Rollie would have gone with Poopsie Wannemaker, his fellow bassoonist in band, while I would have opted for the company of Jerri Hackenbroch or Cheryl Von Tunzelmann. Nonetheless, he and I hunkered down in his room for the long, hard slog to midnight while our parents played bridge and swilled vodka martinis downstairs.

I had tried to engage him in one of the games he owned—Stratego, chess, Battleship—but he'd been yelled at by his dad earlier in the evening and was in a funk. He was always getting yelled at by his dad, which, to my thinking, made it less a reason for falling into funks, it being so ordinary a thing. Rollie, however, didn't see it that way.

I paged joylessly through his five-year-old collection of *Baby Huey* comics while he just sat there on his bed waiting out the Sixties, perhaps hoping that he would turn into a pumpkin at midnight. I always thought of him as more of a tomato, however.

—□—

What did Sophocles or Cocteau imagine that Creon, son of Meneoceus, might look like? This is not clear, apart from the latter's supposed preference for Batgirl masks and pantyhose all around, but it is unlikely that either dramatist envisioned Rollie as the feared and uncontested autocrat of Thebes.

Rollie had earned a slot on the football team through sheer heft, but lacked the killer instinct required for either varsity playing time or ruling besieged city-states. His extracurricular résumé included drama as well, in the form of small roles in big-cast prewar farces that kept him safely on the periphery of the stage. On the plus side, he sported a face well-suited to masked characters.

Given his propensity to quake in the presence of his father, Rollie would have made a crackerjack Hymen, although a reversal of our father-and-son roles would have made for an awkward sight gag seeing as Rollie dwarfed me in every physical dimension. Where was good old Boner when one needed him? You'd think he was born to play Hymen to my Creon, but Mrs. Battersby had relegated him to the role of a stuttering and sycophantic "Guard."

"Enough time wasted! Guards!" yipped Rollie, as Creon, to Boner et al. "Arrest these women! The bravest flee when death approaches!" He had a way of delivering even the most pompous of lines with the whimper of a boy who has just found the freezer devoid of Chocolate Chip Ripple.

The bravest also flee when Mrs. B approaches, which is probably why she normally directed us from a seat in the back row of the auditorium. This only slightly reduced the urge to flee, however, especially in Rollie's case, since he wasn't brave to begin with and proved a dreadful actor to boot. And booting him would have been near the top of Mrs. B's agenda had she allowed herself to get within kicking range.

"*Creon!* When are you gonna learn your *goddam lines!*" "*Creon! Stop fidgeting!*" "*Project*, Creon! *Project!*" "I *still* can't *heeeear* you, *Creeeeeeeeeeon!*"

—◻—

Come the night of our one and only performance, Rollie sucked it up. As I sat at stage left in the pool of my cape, I sensed a change in him that evening, as though he had been born again, finding his inner Creon instead of Jesus.

Gone was the whimper in his imperial decrees. Gone were the squirming and the fidgeting. Only a few of his lines were slow to emerge, and never so slow as to rouse the prompter. He even doled out tongue-twisters like "If you don't show me the guilty parties, you'll soon be declaring that ill-begotten gains bring nothing but pain!" with relative aplomb.

When I showed up and started mouthing off, there ensued this exchange...

Creon: You shall never marry her alive!

Hymen: Then I'll marry her dead—in the underworld!

…which goes to show as well as any other part of our scene together that there is not a single scrap of early Greek tragedy that cannot be rendered preposterous when recited by a big, chubby Midwestern wussie and a scrawny, little one.

"Slave to women, beware! Do not drive me crazy with your tongue-wagging!" Rollie boomed in an almost regal fashion.

"*You* talk all the time and listen to no one!" I protested, prompting him to retort:

"Ha! Is that how things are? Soldiers, bring in the madwoman! Bring in the madwoman! Quick! Quick! That she may die before the eyes of her betrothed!"

But snippy little Hymen was not having any of that. I flipped Rollie off with a cool "This is the last time I speak with you. Farewell. Exercise your rage before your courtiers; *they* will put up with it," before trotting off for my final belly-flop, to the expected scattered guffaws of the jocks in the upper rows.

"That was great! Well done, all!" enthused Mrs. B back in the band room while sad and homely freshman girls scraped off our makeup. "Creon! I'm proud of you!" she added, prompting Rollie's ever-coiled sphincter to relax to previously untested extremes.

"I have a surprise for you," she then added. "I've been negotiating with some people at my college to have us stage the play there! It'll be a week from next Tuesday. I've already made arrangements to get you all out of class!" At which news, Rollie came fearfully close to plunging through his own rectum and hanging himself.

— ☐ —

The Farnsworth College performance is a big event. Big enough, it appears, for a jarringly sudden shift of the narrative into present tense.

On this day of infamy, the entire cast is packed into a convoy consisting of Mrs. Battersby's car and mine. We set out for a school that is just a thirty-minute drive from Mortonville and yet a world away culturally.

From behind the curtain of the Farnsworth auditorium, we hear our jaded bohemian audience trickling in and seating themselves, coughing and murmuring. My overheated imagination pictures them wearing berets and tie-dyed shirts and sitting on the floor in clusters around hookahs, but a quick peak reveals it to be just an ordinary theater, albeit one considerably more intimate than ours, rapidly filling to capacity with students unremarkable but for the prevalence of long and unpermed hair. I am scanning for braless women when our director bursts in.

"Remember that the stage is smaller, so adjust your steps accordingly," gushes a flushed and grinning Mrs. B., obviously stoked to be back on home turf. "I'll be out in the audience. You'll be *great!* Oh, and Creon? *Project!*"

And so our mentor melts into the crowd, probably in hopes of finding a seat from which she can shoot her hypothetical rival— the smarmy, doubting, cigarette-holder-sucking Hermoine—an occasional smirk. But suddenly she reemerges backstage to add, "And remember—there's no prompter."

—◻—

Early on, it becomes clear that Rollie has not brought his A Game today. In fact, it's safe to say that Rollie left all he had on the stage of the Mortonville High auditorium ten days earlier. The Creon that the Farnsworth audience sees is a fidgety Creon, a stuttering Creon, a Creon whose pantyhose at any moment might sag under the weight of a bowel movement as dense as his head.

From the pool that I form with my cape I can feel an oven heat radiating from Rollie, or so it seems. I slowly realize that Rollie is not generating this heat himself but merely conducting it, the actual source of it being Mrs. B out there in Row Thirteen, slowly building toward supernova in her inability to articulate her rage.

Creon's interview with Antigone and Ismene begins. This scene is awkward by nature, since the women have been caught trying to bury their brother's body against Creon's express order, but it takes on new layers of awkwardness not intended by Sophocles when Rollie's lines become progressively shorter and more halting. He is supposed to greet Ismene's entrance in a vicious mood:

Ah! There you are, viper! Come along, speak! Did you or did you not know of the high treason that has been committed?

...which Rollie abridges to "Ah... Speak."

Finally the Chorus chimes in with a cheery paean to Zeus, after which Creon is supposed to give me my cue:

My son, you know the crime and the sentence. Do you come to us as a rebel? Or are we still as dear to you?

But this inquiry is not forthcoming for several beats. Rollie doesn't give me the time of day, not so much as a plain old "Ah...Speak."

Clearly, the adding-an-out-of-town-date-to-our-theatrical-run situation is developing not necessarily to Rollie's advantage. I decide to go on with my visit anyway.

"I bow to your will. After your wise council, there can be no question of marriage," I say, after which we are supposed to exchange our respective longest speeches, with Creon going first. Instead, I hear only a labored, sickly wheeze emit from Rollie. It is accompanied by the rapid and random darting of his eyes, which finally settle on me.

There ensues the following high-speed telepathic exchange between us.

Whisper my lines to me, Josh! Just give me the first few words! A syllable! A syllable! My kingdom for a syllable!

At that moment I flash back to a cookout our families held two summers ago at the Ruegseggers'. Rollie had somehow come into the possession of Jarts, the enormous, insanely unsafe lawn darts that were still a decade away from discovery by the Consumer Product Safety Commission, and we had genuinely enjoyed terrorizing squirrels together for ten minutes or so until his dad barked at us to put those damn things away.

Half an hour later, though, he squandered what goodwill he had earned by ostentatiously chewing his burger with his mouth wide open and then laughing at me when I barfed all over the kitchen table.

It is this memory that rests foremost in my mind as Rollie awaits a reply to his telepathic plea. I give him one: *To heck with you, Rollie.*

Rather than just stand there and stare at him, I decide to go forward with my own speech if only to propel the play forward. There are others, notably Jerri/Ismene, to think about.

The next phase of the scene is a Socratic dialogue, Creon thrusting forth questions for Hymen to parry. This part is a bit trickier to pull off with Rollie still evidently on strike for shorter working hours. That Hymen's answers make no sense without Creon's questions may be registering with some in the audience— these Farnsworth kids are notoriously sharp, after all—but one can hope that Rollie's silence might be interpreted by some as a stern father withholding his affection. Finally, however, we reach an impasse when Hymen says: "*You* talk all the time and listen to no one!"

This, the careful reader will recall, is where Rollie is supposed to command his soldiers to "bring in the madwoman! Quick! Quick!" but at this moment a confrontation with the Mad Woman is the last thing Rollie wants; it is, indeed, the very thing he most wishes he could postpone. He remains mute. He wishes he could somehow fast-forward through this play, through its aftermath, through the rest of his high school career and yes, his entire corporeal life, but in fact time has *slowwwwed downwwwwn.*

"Eh, Creon? Is that how things are? Anyone…anyone you want brought in?"

Still nothing from the robe-swathed fudgesicle that was once my childhood playmate.

"Oh, so you won't talk, eh?"

Rollie doesn't bite at this. Instead he bites at his lower lip.

"Then farewell, father. Exercise your rage before your courtiers. And good luck with that."

As I splatter myself upon these alien boards, the skidding of my torso will be the last sound to emit from the stage but for a few scattered *urp*-like utterances that pop from Rollie's lips as the seconds slowly tick away.

It is a shame that Rollie can't at least summon up Creon's final speech, the one he delivers upon hearing that both his son and wife have killed themselves...

Help! Take me away! Take me away from here! I am less than nothing, less than nothing! I do not know where to look. I do not know where to put my hands, my feet. Everything is going, slipping from under me. A thunderbolt is falling on my head.

...for that would certainly pack his actual thoughts at this moment into a neat little nutshell.

Alas, instead of hearing this haunting lamentation, the audience will see the curtains close at a high speed, passing perilously close to my head with a baleful *whoosh*. For the first time in the two and a half millennia of *Antigone*'s performance history, the title character will not be the one who is put to death offstage.

— □ —

I suppose sensitive readers will resent me for having abandoned Rollie so callously there under the hot stage lights without so much as a syllable of help, an offense that I have now compounded as a writer by leaving him, in the reader's mind, permanently stranded there in the dark behind the curtain, dozens of miles from home, with Donna Battersby closing in on him.

Believe me, I would gruntle you with an uplifting coda to the *Antigone* story if I could do it without bending the truth, but… Well, suffice it to say that as a wussie myself, I simply cannot deal with what happened to Rollie next. It is best left to the gentle reader's imagination.

I can, at least, tell you this: Life went on for Rollie. He married and he had children, none of whom he named Donna or Creon. He established a successful small business in the Mortonville area and has commanded a far better income throughout his career than I have. Not that I've done all that badly, either, mind you. Sure, I have to pay my own wife for sex and POD companies for getting my books into print, but the take-home point here is that I have the disposable income to do those things.

Such being the case, Rollie and I could reunite on stage today—provided he's generous enough to overlook that crack about his face being suited for masked roles—and stand before the world as living proof that the Meek just might inherit the earth after all. Probably not until the Arrogant have depleted all its resources, submerged its coastal cities, and rendered its atmosphere permanently beige, mind you.

But you know what? If I dare speak on behalf of Rollie and Boner and Mr. Black and Mamoru and Edward and Artie and Chet Chudswell and all the rest of our tribe, I guess we'd take it anyway.

If that's all right with the rest of you, that is.

People Who, Through No Fault of Their Own, Helped Me Write This Book

To be sure, the more conventional and concise title for this blurb is "Acknowledgments," but as a wussie and a gentleman I'm leery of giving the wrong impression. It's the rare bird indeed who wants to see his or her real name associated with this sort of book, after all—Lord knows *I* sure don't—and doesn't "acknowledging" someone sort of, well, finger them as an accessory?

I mean, let's suppose that you're Herbert P. Bix. You're brilliant, erudite, and respected by peers for your Pulitzer Prize-winning biography of Hirohito. You're sitting in your den one morning in your tweed blazer, tranquilly puffing away on your calabash pipe, when in steams your secretary all atwitter.

"Oh, Professor Bix!" she burbles, "You've just been acknowledged by an author named Muggins!"

"Ah, capital! Capital!" you say, as this is how I imagine Pulitzer Prize-winning biographers talk. "But…what was that name?"

"Muggins."

"The Devil you say. Muggins? Muggins? What an odd name. And therefore all the odder that I don't remember conferring with any Muggins. Refresh my memory, my dear: Who or what exactly is Professor Muggins's subject?"

"Wussies!"

"Eh? What's that, Betsy? I thought you said *wussies*."

"The full title is *Wussie: In Praise of Spineless Men*."

"Why, this is really quite extraordinary!"

"This Muggins person cites your Hirohito biography as a vital source for the chapter in which he compares the Showa emperor to—ah yes, here is the phrase—'that dorky, forgettable second cousin who shows up in your dorm one hungover Sunday morning with a note from your mom pinned to his chest.'"

There ensues a life-threatening three-minute coughing fit, which is followed hard-upon by a recap of the above exchange, in turn followed by a command for Betsy to ring up all the solicitors chop-chop. And so things roll rapidly downhill between Professor Bix and me from there on out.

Now I realize that writers these days do tend to pad their Acknowledgments pages with shout-outs to persons with whom they have had no contact in the course of writing their books—to heroes who provided inspiration, musicians whose melodies helped them unwind after a hard day at the keyboard, that sort of thing. God, for one, is always managing to get Himself sucked into the fray somehow; but having pressed my luck with Him a number of times in these pages already, I think it prudent to leave Him out of the Acknowledgments.

Alas, I cannot in good faith let Herbert P. Bix off the hook quite so easily, because I did read his book, *Hirohito: The Making of Modern Japan*. And since I couldn't make heads or tails out of it, I read it again. On the Impenetrable Prose Stylist Scale, I place Bix about halfway between Elizabeth Wurtzel and Henry David Thoreau.

Eventually, though, and entirely without his meaning to do so, Bix did provide me with tons of useful insights for the writing of my Hirohito chapter. So did Leonard Mosley, the presumably forgiving, presumably gracious, and presumably very dead author of the much earlier and more obscure *Hirohito, Emperor of Japan*. Of course, the tenor and thesis of my chapter are entirely my own, as are the inevitable errors.

Chief among those whose names I must defile by noting their wholly inadvertent helping hands with my Thomas Jefferson chapter is the estimable Joseph J. Ellis, author of *American Sphinx: The Character of Thomas Jefferson* and *Founding Brothers: The Revolutionary Generation*. But the equally blameless Annette Gordon-Reed (*The Hemingses of Monticello*) and David McCullough (*John Adams*) cannot be left out, just as it ought to go without saying that Christopher Hitchens (*Thomas Jefferson: Author of America*) could not conceivably have had anything less to do with the writing of this book.

All of the above are guiltless of the inaccuracies that no doubt honeycomb my writing, and I assure you that there is no truth to the rumor that these superb scholars have ever "palled around with" literary terrorists like me.

Bruce Feiler's *Abraham: A Journey to the Heart of Three Faiths* was indispensable to my chapter on Isaac, but don't you dare go laying that at his doorstep.

Similarly, Robert D. Richardson, Jr., author of *Thoreau: A Life of the Mind*, bears no responsibility for my take on the famed Concord Moss-Eater, though it's true just the same that I could never have made much headway without him.

On a more personal level, I can dare to hope that Gary Pettis and Bill "Badlands" Utermohlen will not object too strenuously to my thanking them here for their critical input, advice, and encouragement as well as for their enduring friendship.

And Mrs. Muggins, of course, always merits all the gratitude and love than I can humanly muster for leaving me alone to write the sort of drivel that keeps me in some semblance of sanity. She really doesn't know about the *ex-say oy-tay*, by the way, so let's keep that among ourselves, shall we? I'm running out of drawers.

Obligatory Disclaimer.

This book is a work of fiction. Names, characters, and incidents either are the products of the author's imagination or are used fictitiously. Any resemblance to actual events, organizations, or persons, living or dead, is entirely coincidental and beyond the intent of the author. If waterboarded, I am apt to confess that the personal anecdotes in this book are largely factual, or at least my best attempt at recollecting the past. But no expert on torture puts much stock in such confessions, nor should you.

Photo and illustration credits

Illustrations "Honolulu Bus Schematic," "Wussie-Fruity-Gay Venn Diagram," and "USIA Reading Room Cleavage Viewing Zone" by Gary Pettis.

Photo of Laurent de La Hyre's "Abraham Sacrificing Isaac" from Wikipedia Commons. Commons is a freely licensed media file repository.

Photo by US Army photographer Lt. Gaetano Faillace of Emperor Hirohito and General Douglas MacArthur at their first meeting at the US Embassy, Tokyo, 27 September, 1945 from Wikipedia Commons. Commons is a freely licensed media file repository.

Photo of John Wilkes Booth, Edwin Booth and Junius Booth, Jr. (from left to right) in Shakespeare's *Julius Caesar* in 1864 from Wikipedia Commons. Commons is a freely licensed media file repository.

Photo of Charles Willson Peale's portrait of Thomas Jefferson (Philadelphia, 1791) from Wikipedia Commons. Commons is a freely licensed media file repository.

Photo by villy of Henry David Thoreau in June 1856 (aged 39) from Wikipedia Commons. Commons is a freely licensed media file repository.

Photo "Wookies" by Narno available under a Creative Commons Attribution-Share Alike license.

Photo of schoolboys and teacher by NSW available under a Creative Commons Generic Attribution license.

www.ingramcontent.com/pod-product-compliance
Lightning Source LLC
Chambersburg PA
CBHW030919090426
42737CB00007B/251